101

PLACES TO
VISIT

Not

101 PLACES NOT TO VISIT

ADAM RUSS

ROBSON
BOOKS

Produced 2008 by
Salamander Books
10 Southcombe Street
London W14 0RA
An imprint of Anova Books Company Ltd

First published in Great Britain in 2005 by
Robson Books
10 Southcombe Street
London W14 0RA
An imprint of Anova Books Company Ltd

© 2005 PRC Publishing

4 5 6 7 8 9

ISBN: 978-1-86105-858-4

Printed in Singapore

Contents

Introduction

Why Leave Home?

Staying at home is the natural state for the modern man, woman or child. Face it. Think about where you would choose to spend your time if you suddenly stopped needing to go to work. In fact, think back to that day off you took last week because of that terrible bug that was doing the rounds and you thought you could get away without producing a doctor's note. What did you do with your day off? Hit the library? Treat yourself to that art gallery outing you've been promising yourself for the last quarter century? No, you stayed at home. And you were right to do so. The desire to go outside is born of a restless mind, and a restless mind is an affliction for which a nice lie down is the best possible remedy.

Despite this, the travel industry continues to achieve record profits. Every year, otherwise rational people spend their hard earned cash on being transported to parts of the planet they have no connection with, little understanding of and which they very rarely appreciate.

What follows is an essential travel guide for people who hate to travel. We all have to leave the house sometimes – unless we're lucky enough to have one of those electronic tags on our leg – but listed here, in no ranking order of vileness, are 101 places you should by all means possible avoid. The fact that your own dreary suburb or feral wasteland isn't listed here should not be taken as any recommendation, as chances are it's probably a complete dump. But the cities described here are frequently ones on the list of any would-be-traveller. Also included are places that pose a continued threat to the existence of anyone moronic enough to enter their borders.

This book is for people who've had enough. Travel is exhausting, expensive, dangerous and frequently unsanitary. Jesus didn't go on holiday, unless you count his city break in Jerusalem. And we all know how that worked out for him.

10 Jobs to Be Avoided at all Costs – and Where to Avoid Doing Them

1) East European Food Taster
"Mmm, and that's got just a hint of coriander in it, comrade chairman. Or is it strychnine?"

2) Mini Bus Driver – Anywhere
The officially-recognised, statistically-assured most dangerous way to travel. A thought worth bearing in mind next time you sign release forms for your kids' school outings.

3) Traffic Warden in London
Universally reviled but probably the only thing that's stopping London from looking like Calcutta in drizzly monochrome.

4) Honest Cop anywhere in South America
"A party to welcome me to the department? That's great. I knew Pepe and Chico would come round to my way of thinking. The old cement factory on the outskirts of town? Sounds great. What time?"

5) Bicycle Courier in Madrid
Like most Westerners, the Spanish hate anyone going faster than them in traffic. And they're already homicidal drivers to begin with. Why give them an excuse?

6) Electrician in Delhi
Who needs fancy rubber handled screwdrivers when there's perfectly good cutlery to hand?

7) Professional Footballer in Colombia
As if having teams of professional assassins watching you more closely than the referee wasn't bad enough, the recent lightning bolts directed at Colombia's national squad seem to suggest they've now got the manager in the big dugout upstairs angry about something.

8) Toilet Cleaner in Egypt
Pharaoh gets his revenge both on you and on the poor sap that gets to clean up after you're done.

9) Timeshare Salesman in the Middle East
"…And since the air strikes brought down the other half of the street you've got yourself a fantastic view of the oil refinery."

10) UN Peacekeeper
Your tank is white. Your helmet is powder blue. And you need to get signed consent forms from those attacking you before you fire back.

LET'S NOT GO TO...

Africa

EXPECT TO HEAR AN AFRICAN SAY:
"When is it our turn?"

MOST OBVIOUS LOW POINTS:
Poverty, civil war, dangerous creatures

SLIGHT COMPENSATIONS:
Cheap cost of living, friendly people, safari

OVERALL RATING: ★

★★★★★	**ANIMALTASTIC**
★★★★	**JUNGLE FEVER**
★★★	**HAKUNA MATATA**
★★	**SAFARI SUITS**
★	**(GET) OUT OF AFRICA**

Bujumbura

The ongoing tribal war between Hutus and Tutsis gives Bujumbura the feel of a community production of *West Side Story*, with more fights, no dance routines and a cast of around two million.

Country: Burundi	
Boredom Rating	★★★
Likelihood of Fatal Visit	★★★★
Essential Packing	Quart of your own blood type
Most Likely Cause of Death	Gunshot wound – if you're very, very lucky

History

Once upon a time there was a beautiful little country nestled between Tanzania, Rwanda and Zaire. The land had many beautiful snow-capped mountains that offered spectacular views over Lake Tanganyika – which was just as well, as the race that lived there were pygmies, and as a result generally had trouble seeing two feet in front of them over the high grass on the plains. However, the Twa – as the native people were known – were peaceful and home loving, and sadly doomed as a result. Displaced by migrating Hutu farmers, the Twa are still clinging onto existence but now make up a mere one percent of the country's population. However, the Hutus were themselves subjugated by the Tutsi tribesmen that arrived from Uganda and Ethiopia in the 16th century. The Tutsi offered the Hutu a once-in-a-lifetime opportunity to trade their land and labour for livestock. Momentarily forgetting that the livestock aren't in the habit of either taking themselves to market or hovering in space, the Hutus got stiffed on the deal and have been understandably pissed off ever since.

Culture

You'd think that the inherent hatred the two dominant tribes feel for each other would spill over into Burundi's culture, but this is surprisingly not the case. Like the best dysfunctional families all over the world, the people of Burundi are doing their utmost to pretend to the outside world that everything is alright. Even in the capital city of Bujumbura, the hapless citizens are putting on their best smiles and visibly seeming grateful to be living in a country where genocide is the number one national sport. This wasn't very easy to do when the army were driving truckloads of dismembered bodies through the streets everyday. But it's got a lot easier since they started scheduling their convoys of death to make their rounds at three o'clock in the morning.

The Belgian Empire

Germany's attempts to colonise the country at the turn of the 20th century were so lame that even the Belgians managed to get the better of them during World War I. The legacy of Belgium's one notable instance of empire building is a country so riven by tribal racism and hatred it makes the rest of the planet look like the video for a Paul McCartney duet.

Attractions

Not surprisingly, anything of any value that once existed in downtown Bujumbura has been long since smashed, shot to bits or looted. This makes a visit to the Musée Vivant on Avenue du 13 Octobre an experience of terminal tedium even by the standards set by other African museums. However, the museum does boast a reconstruction of a traditional Burundian village, which should prove useful as a template for all the new villages that'll need rebuilding should the conflict that still engulfs the country ever come to an end.

Local Tip No.43: Never stare at a brick carrier, even if his load is fascinatingly wobbly.

Eating and Drinking

The ferocity of the ongoing tribal warfare has meant that the few hotels and private houses still standing are all full of relief workers and foolhardy foreign correspondents. Although this means that you've got little chance of finding an open restaurant or anywhere indoors to sleep, at least the lions and tigers in Burundi are eating well.

Cape Town

Since Nelson's release, Cape Town has sought to become rich in opportunity for both black and white South Africans. So far it's got it half right.

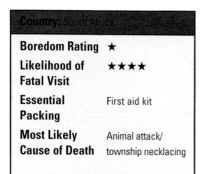

Country: South Africa	
Boredom Rating	★
Likelihood of Fatal Visit	★★★★
Essential Packing	First aid kit
Most Likely Cause of Death	Animal attack/ township necklacing

History

Perhaps no country in the world has served as more of a crucible for the socio-political shifts of the latter half of the 20th century than South Africa. And no South African city better represents the contrast between old guard and new order than Cape Town. Fortunately, the pace of change throughout the country has been remarkable, and Cape Town is at the cutting edge of this change. Black and white South Africans mingle easily in their capital city, free to choose to live and work where they please. That most of the indigenous population opt for careers in catering, cleaning and refuse collection merely reflects their comfort in such roles and their continued reliance on an elite, privately educated, white-collar class to take on the challenge and responsibilities of roles in finance, administration and corporate management.

Culture

Despite the best efforts of the well-motivated and highly tolerant police force, crime has been a recurring problem throughout Cape Town's history. However, visitors to Cape Town should feel confident to stroll the streets, providing they follow a few simple rules. They need to stay on busy main streets, make sure they are accompanied by an armed bodyguard at all times, and leave valuable items such as jewellery, cash, leather shoes and clothing with zips stowed safely in the hotel.

Attractions

Once you've toured the townships, been held up at gunpoint on the beach and left hanging for two hours in the sun in a faulty cable car on the way to the top of the Table Mountain, you might think that you'd experienced everything that Cape Town has to offer in the thrill-seeking department. But you'd be wrong. The Cape of Good Hope has been recognised as one of the most unpredictable patches of ocean on the planet, and should therefore be an essential part of any adrenaline-junkie's itinerary. Boats of all sizes and in varying states of repair are readily available for charter at Victoria Wharf, and the choppiness of the seas means that even the most experienced of yachtsmen will be put to the test just in staying afloat. Those souls unfortunate enough to be washed overboard in the face of such perilous conditions may draw comfort from the fact that they are ensured a relatively quick release from this mortal coil. If the near-Arctic water temperatures don't bring on a terminal case of exposure and a delirious death, then one of the great white sharks roaming off the coast will soon ensure an end that is mercifully quicker.

Eating and Drinking

Like much of Africa, Cape Town has an incredibly diverse variety of exotic animals, ranging from Jackass Penguins to Emus and Springbok. All of these can be seen up close even in downtown Cape Town simply by wandering into any good restaurant and ordering a selection of the day's specials.

Signposts are everywhere in Cape Town, helping to remind visitors and residents alike that if it's any fun you can't do it.

Casablanca

Q: How do you separate the men from the boys in Morocco?

A: With a bucket of cold water.

Country: Morocco	
Boredom Rating	★
Likelihood of Fatal Visit	★★★
Essential Packing	Bribe money
Most Likely Cause of Death	Faulty hookah

History

Of all the cities in Africa, and possibly the entire world, Casablanca is the travel destination most associated with mystery and romance. But wherever Bogart, Bergman and the Epstein brothers drew their inspiration from, it's safe to say it wasn't the actual Casablanca, a city with little to recommend it to anyone for whom romance is not allocated on an hourly rate. While other parts of Morocco are more famous for sex tourism, there's still plenty of it going on in Casablanca, which doesn't even serve up its vice with the nice backdrops of Marrakesh.

Culture

Any traveller who makes it to Casablanca in one piece is assured a warm welcome, which they should on no account be taken in by. Trust no one, keep moving at all costs and don't bother to waste time looking for decent-quality accommodation since there is none to be found anyway.

Romance and mystery are part and parcel of downtown Casablanca.

Sealing the Deal

Once you've finished haggling, settling on a wildly inappropriate price for a pile of stuff you didn't want in the first place, and you've secured the release of any friends or family who unwittingly got included in the bargaining process, you'll want to arrange to send your goods home. For security reasons you'll need to take ID to the post office, such as your passport. Postage is very cheap in Morocco, but convincing the postmaster that's it's worth his while to sell you back your passport can be expensive, however.

Attractions

Head to the Medina (ancient quarter) for a shopping experience unlike anything you've ever known. The Berbers – a Hamitic tribe that are spread all over North Africa – have transformed the purchase of a few souvenir trinkets into an exchange that bears more of a resemblance to a police interrogation. Accepting the invitation to share a cup of mint tea will quickly lead to a casual discussion of the quality of the rugs on offer which will itself lead to an impressive mountain of merchandise being piled up on your behalf. Attempt to explain in a calm fashion that you are travelling light and the fun will really start. Beg the Berbers to calm down and insist that you had no intention of offending the quality of their stock or family name and the haggling can begin.

Eating and Drinking

Cheap cafes and restaurants are in abundance in Casablanca, and in contrast to many parts of the world, smoking is considered an essential and highly sociable part of dining. Cigars, cigarettes, pipes and hookahs are prevalent, many filled with substances stronger than mere tobacco, and once you've sampled Moroccan cuisine you'll understand why.

Harare

With the rise of barmy white power nationalist groups across Europe and the former Soviet Union, it's nice to see Zimbabwe making a late bid for title of most racist country on the planet.

Country: Zimbabwe	
Boredom Rating	★★
Likelihood of Fatal Visit	★★★★
Essential Packing	Black greasepaint
Most Likely Cause of Death	Voting for anyone but Mugabe

History

The settlement of Great Zimbabwe, one of the great civilisations, dates back to the early 11th century, when the Bantu tribes forcibly enlisted the indigenous Khoisan settlers in their agricultural and gold-mining plans for the region. By the 15th century, Zimbabwe had become one of the most densely populated parts of Africa. Tribal rivalries prevented it from becoming the first African super state, and after fracturing into a number of tribal fiefdoms, it became vulnerable to the inevitable wave of missionaries, explorers and freeloaders from Europe looking to civilise the continent with their unique combination of cricket, Christianity and summary execution for anyone who disagreed with them.

Culture

Now in his 80s – and, by the looks of things, still going strong – President Robert Mugabe has managed to hang onto power since Zimbabwe attained independence and a new name in 1980. On paper, his Marxist dictatorship has been a remarkable success. However, this may be because Mugabe owns the paper and has the editor's daughter held hostage. His control of the state-run media is vice-like to a degree that even Rupert Murdoch would blanch at and is merely one of the many leashes Mugabe keeps on his increasingly isolated nation. And while it is unlikely that he will ever achieve his ambition of a one-party state in Zimbabwe, his electoral rivals are generally kept pretty busy with harassment from Harare's notorious law-and-order branch of the police, not to mention keeping up to date with boundary changes. As a result, their campaigns tend to have all the staying power of a crane fly under a windscreen wiper.

Attractions

Economic sanctions imposed on Zimbabwe have led to increases in unemployment, inflation, crime and the number of first-class air trips Mrs. Grace Mugabe has to take to Europe regularly to stock up on shoes. Expect to have your wallet stolen and you are unlikely to be disappointed.

The National Gallery of Zimbabwe is a popular spot, and the muggers who operate on this patch will often be happy to give you a brief talk on whichever work you happen to be in front of when they rob you, for no extra charge. However depressing you may find Harare, resist the urge to head out into the country unless you have a pressing reason to do so and/or an armed escort. The gangs of armed men who roam the countryside and suburbs taking possession of land, vehicles or anything else that catches their eye may not be professional killers, but on recent evidence they're clearly very gifted amateurs.

Eating and Drinking

What happens when you take the kind of tasteless slop the English passed off as food 100 years or so ago and build it around a base of the maize porridge that all but the privileged elite of Zimbabwe exist on? No-one seems to be too sure, but that's all that's on offer in Harare unless you're able to blag your way into one of the premier's dinner parties. Anaesthetise yourself before you order with a bucket or two of *chibuku* beer and avoid the chicory-rich coffee unless a mouthful of dirt is your idea of a taste sensation.

A government-commisioned survey has revealed that most Zimbabweans appreciate the leisure time afforded them by not working, going to school or eating.

Rhodes – A Diamond Geezer

The most successful English invader was Cecil John Rhodes. His dreams of transforming the continent into a civilisation that Queen Victoria could be proud of were hindered only by the presence of so many Africans with visions for their nation that didn't necessarily involve the English ordering them about. The country that Rhodes gave his name to was a civilised society rich in opportunity for the many white settlers who headed there at the end of the 19th century and an oppressive dictatorship for everyone else. Laws designed to favour the causes of white colonialists fed the fires of resistance and helped to create the conditions for the mess the country is now in.

Khartoum

The West has certainly done all it can to help Sudan, flying out consignments of weapons even in the most hazardous of conditions.

Country:	Sudan
Boredom Rating	★★★
Likelihood of Fatal Visit	★★★★
Essential Packing	Bio Protection Suit
Most Likely Cause of Death	Virus that'll affect more than just your hard drive

Many passengers like to pray while they are aboard the city's ferries, a practice that is generally encouraged by the ship's crew.

History

Built on the southern bank of the Nile as a military outpost in 1821, Khartoum was named after the thin ridge of land between the Blue and White Niles, which resembled a *khurtum*, or elephant's trunk. The town grew fat on the profits of the slave trade and its rapid expansion led to European colonisation. Lord Kitchener rebuilt the city and had the strange idea of laying out streets in the shape of the Union Jack. The Egyptian residents of the region put up with British intervention, at least until two world wars were out of the way, at which point their hunger to determine their own future, or lack thereof, became too powerful to resist. They celebrated their independence by splitting along religious lines and embarking on a civil war that successive political leaders have been unable or unwilling to stop.

Culture

The Sudanese Ambassador to London has recently demanded to know why the cancer-causing dye at the centre of a major food scare in the UK is named after his beloved homeland. He has expressed his concern that the choice of nomenclature could do damage to the image of the war-torn, ebola-ridden disaster area of which he is blessed with the honour of being envoy. Missing the point on such a grand scale is central to Sudanese culture.

Attractions

While the birthplace of the Ebola virus is yet to be established, the first reported case was in the Sudan. This makes Khartoum a fascinating place for biologists and viral specialists, but somewhere to be avoided by everyone else. The Ethnographical Museum contains examples of musical instruments, clothes and other household items that date back some 200 years, but also represent the cutting edge of Sudanese design. Identical items are available for sale at the general provisions store next door.

Eating and Drinking

The lack of tourists in Khartoum means that there will be no danger of you being fobbed off with Westernised muck – whatever food you're lucky to come across will be authentic Sudanese muck.

Britain's Most Wanting Man

Lord Kitchener's reputation as a military strategist was sealed by the Battle of Omdurman in 1898. Kitchener and his troops bravely faced the onslaught of locals armed with spears and rocks with only several regiments of men and a consignment of Gatlings and Maxim belt-fed machine guns.

Mogadishu

Pack your cares away and say goodbye to everyday woes. Come to Somalia and soon you won't have a problem in the world – well this world anyway.

Country: Somalia	
Boredom Rating	★★★★
Likelihood of Fatal Visit	★★★★★
Essential Packing	Burial instructions
Most Likely Cause of Death	The mine with your name on it

History

When even a bunch of hardcore, no-fear, hippy hedonists like the people at Lonely Planet issue warnings to anyone considering a trip there, you know there's a very serious problem with the place. Lonely Planet has been advising travellers where to head for the ultimate (travel) highs since 1973 and is renowned for not letting minor disturbances such as civil wars or natural disasters come between its cadre and the best (chemically enhanced) times to be had on the planet.

But in this case they're right to be cautious. Every now and then the statistics don't lie, and Somalia is officially one of the three most dangerous places to be in the world, along with Chechnya and Iraq. This leaves it somewhat in the middle with regard to US policy: Chechnya is a problem the US wishes it could get involved with but probably can't and shouldn't, while Iraq is a problem it shouldn't have started and now probably can't and won't get out of. Wherever Somalia fits in Uncle Sam's global intentions, he's being cagey about it and very little is being done about it at the moment – which is another way of saying the UN are dealing with it. Rumours of plans to simply "bomb back to the Jurassic era" everything along the line of longitude 45 degrees east of where the three locations are located have been strongly denied by the Pentagon.

Culture

As one of the earliest Arab settlements on the East African coast, Somalia has a rich cultural history. The men of the country are largely oblivious to this. Those who aren't busy getting caught up in the constant tribal disputes that provide an endless source of fuel for the ongoing civil war are either hustling their families out of the country at the earliest opportunity or numbing the pain of everyday existence with a few hours of earnest *khat* chewing. Women are viewed as less important than men in Somali society and are therefore not expected to involve themselves in important matters such as cultural affairs. Their job is merely to maintain the home against the never-ending threat of drought and keep dad and the kids fed though the frequent harvest failures and ongoing threat of famine. Despite all this, get the men folk away from the guns and plant stimulants and you'll soon see that they're a great people who put up with a lot and enjoy every minute as if it were their last. Which, statistically speaking for the average Somali, there's a good chance it will be.

Attractions

Mogadishu is blessed with a wealth of attractions you'll be too busy dodging bullets and being held at knifepoint to enjoy. Situated on the longest national

Mogadishu's Landmarks

The most important landmark in Mogadishu is the Arba-Rucun Mosque, or mosque of the four pillars, which can be seen from pretty much anywhere else in the city. Use this to get your bearings back to the hotel so that you can phone your travel agent and ask him why the hell he sold you a ticket to Somalia in the first place.

Despite their fearsome reputation, military personnel in the city are always happy to take a minute and help tourists with whatever they may need.

coastline in Africa, the beach boasts golden sands, a vicious undertow and a resident shark population kept well fed on a regular diet of die-hard surfers.

Eating and Drinking

Head for any restaurant in Mogadishu and you'll find no alcohol and no women. What you will find is a bunch of zonked-out men having interminable discussions in a language you'll struggle to comprehend. In fact, you could easily recreate the atmosphere of a Mogadishu restaurant by going and spending a cheerful afternoon in the nursing home with your grandpa. Now do you really need to hear about the food?

Tangiers

Most travel guides recommend that the best thing you can do on arrival in Tangiers is to make immediate plans to get the hell out, if you've not done so already. And they're right to: Tangiers is truly a hole of the first order.

Country: Morocco	
Boredom Rating	★★★
Likelihood of Fatal Visit	★★★
Essential Packing	Rubber ring
Most Likely Cause of Death	Shipwreck

History

Morocco has long provided an escape route out of Europe, and for anyone heading south into the continent of Africa the arrival on the shores of Tangiers is always a momentous moment and one that truly marks the departure from Western civilisation and into another world altogether. While many commercial airliners have been known to land successfully at Tangiers Airport, the departure lounge has been so besieged by hawkers, beggars and cabbies driving ex-SS Mercedes-Benz estates that no traveller has successfully made it out of the arrivals hall since 1992. Your best bet is to take the ferry from Algeciras in southern Spain – though once you've seen the ferry you may feel that, as bets go, you're probably safer having a little flutter on a couple of rounds of Russian Roulette.

Culture

Tangiers has all the cultural interest of a service-station forecourt, albeit without the handy plastic gloves and tissue dispensers. The only fun to be had is watching the new arrivals get conned out of their earthly possessions, assuming you're not too busy getting shafted yourself. However, Tangiers does offer excellent transport links, meaning you can at least get out quickly. In fact, by this time you'll probably even be considering getting back on the ferry and getting the hell out of Africa altogether. But bear in mind that wherever you head next, you are likely to be seriously delayed by the inevitable full-cavity searches that will accompany your arrival in any customs hall in the world now that your passport bears a fresh Moroccan stamp.

Attractions

Morocco became a part of the hugely popular European Inter-Rail scheme in 1988. Since then countless student backpackers have availed themselves of the opportunity to take a few tentative

Letting the Train Take the Strain

Find the nicest seat you can in the air-conditioned first class carriage and get yourself in the best possible frame of mind for the beating you are guaranteed to receive from whatever team of ticket inspectors happen upon you cluttering up their train – Moroccan railway employees, like Velociraptors, always work in pairs. As you are tossed off the platform onto the tracks, comfort yourself with the knowledge that since all the grant money went on rolling stock, most railway stations in Morocco don't come with a platforms of any description, so your fall is considerably reduced. Bear also in mind that since you are a tourist, the guards are going considerably easier on you than they would on their fellow countrymen.

There are many colourful and varied street cafes where one can stop for a delightful meal. For those visitors in a hurry – why not pick up a terracotta pot noodle.

steps into the enigma of Africa and generous grants have helped to make Moroccan train carriages among the most comfortable you'll ever sit in. However, getting onto the train in the first place may provide you with an entirely different experience. A half-baked rollout of training programmes for Moroccan ticket inspectors, combined with an apparent absence of anywhere to legally buy a ticket, has created an atmosphere of confusion over which tickets are valid on which train. This in turn has led in the past to a few regrettable incidents of violence against customers by ticket inspectors and train guards. Fortunately, the Moroccan railway authority has recognised the problem and has sought to adopt a more uniform approach to Western travellers. As a result, passengers can now expect a consistently aggressive attitude from every railway worker that they meet, be he guard, inspector, cleaner or driver, regardless of the ticket they bear.

Eating and Drinking

Eating and drinking are just two of the activities likely to further infuriate the guards on your train and you are strongly advised not to indulge in either.

Yamoussoukro

The Ivory Coast is aptly named, since there is now a great deal more ivory in the country than there are elephants.

Country: Ivory Coast	
Boredom Rating	★
Likelihood of Fatal Visit	★★★★★
Essential Packing	Last will and testament
Most Likely Cause of Death	Machete attack

History

Wherever you go in the world, some things remain constant, so a healthy sense of neighbourly rivalry is as common in Africa as it is in Europe, Asia or the Americas, regardless of any other cultural differences that may exist. This may explain why the Ivory Coast seems to have worked so hard in recent years to compete with places like Rwanda and Zimbabwe for the title of least-welcoming country on the continent. Anyone considering a trip there should have a lie down. As a general rule, if the missionaries are getting out, you should probably question how vital your trip is. Unless of course you're looking to end it all, in which case the Ivory Coast is probably the place for you.

The French, who controlled the country's economic output through a much-hated forced-labour policy until it gained independence in 1960, have been the targets of the majority of recent attacks. However, the multiracial makeup of modern French society has made it difficult for the machete-wielding mobs to know exactly who they should be attacking. As a result, skin colour is no longer a consideration and anyone who enters the region with two arms and two legs can consider themselves fair game and should not expect to leave the country with the same quota of limbs as they possessed on arrival.

Culture

Yamoussoukro is in many ways a capital city in name only: the home village of President Felix Houphouët-Boigny, the father of independence, the city has had money lavished in all the wrong places. It's this kind of economic acumen that led Houphouët-Boigny to become the first African to become a minister in a European government. The well-lit, eight-lane highway is generally deserted and therefore an excellent venue for picnics and softball games. The Basilique Notre-Dame-de-la-Paix is an almost exact replica of St Peter's in Rome and is the tallest church in all of Christendom, which is probably a real talking point at the coffee mornings for the country's half-dozen or so practising Catholics. At a cost of 300 million US dollars – a sum equalling half the national budget deficit – Ivory Coast has shown its ability to punch above its weight in debt generation, even by Western standards.

Attractions

Unlike many parts of the continent, Ivory Coast has three distinct seasons – a dry and barren spring from November to March; an arid, insufferable summer

Getting There

Recent violence in the capital city has left many buildings vacant and so there is a surplus of accommodation for any traveller hell-bent (and probably heaven-destined) on checking out its delights. Abdijan International Airport has excellent facilities and is located on the coast some 90 miles from Yamoussoukro. Cabs to and from the airport are cheap and easy to find, which is fairly pointless since the only way you'll get a commercial airliner to land there is if you hijack it – which is not unheard of.

Public transport in Yamoussoukro is luxurious. With over thirty goats per passenger, even during rush hour, there is plenty of room to stretch out on a goat, put your feet up on a goat and do the crossword.

from March to May; and a sticky and humid rainy season from June to October. Spring brings the most bearable temperatures, not to mention sandstorms blown by the Harmattan south from the Sahara, which can reduce visibility to a few metres. Take shelter from these in the lush rainforests that surround the city – for the moment at least. Ivory Coast is logging rainforest at a more devastating rate than any other country on earth, so there's no guarantee it'll still be there by the time you read this.

Eating and Drinking

Even in the capital city, food is eaten with the hands – another reason, if you needed one, for trying your best to hang onto both of yours, particularly since in polite African society only the right hand is used at the table. *Attiéké* is a popular dish: a lot like couscous, it's made of grated cassava and is generally served as a side dish – usually to complement a main course of even more *attiéké*. *Bangui* is a local palm wine that is excellent for washing in after a meal.

LET'S NOT GO TO...

The Artic or Antarctica

EXPECT TO HEAR A POLAR BEAR/PENGUIN SAY:
"Brrrr"

MOST OBVIOUS LOW POINTS:
The cold and ice

SLIGHT COMPENSATIONS:
The solitude

OVERALL RATING: ★

FORGET IT. JUST DON'T GO, OK?

Bouvetoya

Do you want ice in that?

Country: South Atlantic Ocean	
Boredom Rating	★
Likelihood of Fatal Visit	★
Essential Packing	Scarf, hat, buttons, carrot and two pieces of coal
Most Likely Cause of Death	Going outside

History

No one knew about it for centuries, even though everyone said it had to be there. Many men died trying to get to the middle of it, but when it was finally reached those who claimed it wasted no time in getting away from it. It remains so unwanted that, despite territorial claims from seven competing nations, a treaty signed in 1961 protecting its status as a place where scientists from all nations can work together in a spirit of international co-operation still remains intact. And if we all keep insisting on having armpits that don't smell like three-day-old road-kill, it may soon not be there at all. The question surely should be not "What can we do to save the Antarctic?" but "Remind me why we'd miss it if it went?"

Culture

Culture on the ice floe at the bottom of the world tends to be homemade. Leave 100 monkeys in a room with 100 typewriters for 100 years and maybe they will come up with a great novel. But leave 1,200 scientists on a continent for nine months with only each other for company and the best you can expect culturally is some Kasparov-standard chess games, a lot of lethal home-brew and a bunch of worn-out VHS copies of the X-Files. Of course, every now and then one or more of the ice geeks may go a bit crazy, shave their eyebrows off and set fire to the base, but other than that you'll have to rely on the act of staying alive in the planet's most inhospitable climate to keep you amused.

Attractions

Bouvetoya has all the attractions you'd expect of the continent as a whole, i.e. none at all, and it also bears the distinction of being the most isolated island on Earth, lying nearly 1,000 miles from any substantial land mass – perfect for getting away from it all, probably for ever. Local land-based wildlife is dominated by a small wingless midge that clearly did something to piss off God in a former life. The island is also notable for being the site of a thermonuclear explosion in 1979, which no nation has ever claimed responsibility for, and which the French disputed the veracity of readings on, claiming it wasn't an armaments detonation but merely a severe bowel movement being experienced by a passing blue whale.

Eating and Drinking

If you're going to run out of supplies, December and January are probably the months to do so as the early summer weather heralds the arrival of courting penguins. While these may not be as easy to eat as the biscuits bearing their name, they are at least free from artificial colourings and preservatives.

Before you go, you'll think one ice flow looks just like another. By the time you come back, you just won't care.

LET'S NOT GO TO...

Asia

EXPECT TO HEAR AN ASIAN SAY:
"We're next"

MOST OBVIOUS LOW POINTS:
Earthquakes, alien languages, sweatshops

SLIGHT COMPENSATIONS:
Remarkable landscapes, high proportion of
English speakers, cheap electronic goods

OVERALL RATING: ★

★★★★★   **BOMBAY DREAMS**

★★★★   **ASIAN TIGER**

★★★   **CHINA DOLL**

★★   **FENG-SHUI FUSSY**

★   **NOT FOR ALL THE TEA IN CHINA**

Astana

Astana's combination of remoteness, spiralling prices, extreme weather and utter pointlessness make it a destination that appeals to only the most chronically moronic of travellers.

Country: Kazakhstan	
Boredom Rating	★★★★
Likelihood of Fatal Visit	★★
Essential Packing	Bucket and spade
Most Likely Cause of Death	(Mis-)guided missile

History

The Kazakhs have had an interesting journey through history. Once at the centre of the empires of both Alexander the Great and Genghis Khan, they then became the personal guinea pigs for a generation of Soviet economists, social engineers and rocket scientists. They currently reside in the "where are they now file?" Many political strategists have located the region as being central in determining where international power will shift in the course of the next century, but up till now these experts have

Kazakh Poetry Recitals

Like the majority of nomadic cultures, the Kazakhs hold the oral tradition in great esteem – though get close enough to one and you'll quickly realise that they hold the concept of oral hygiene far less highly. A night's entertainment in Astana is likely to climax with an *aity*, a contested recital between two poets that's a lot like a freestyle rap battle with a six-hour running time and no microphones, crotch-grabbing or references to your opponent's immediate family allowed.

been remarkably quiet about just why that is. The Silk Road through central-eastern Asia – so key to the development of trade from the time that BC became AD – has long been the personal fiefdom of the Golden Triangle of Drug Lords from South East Asia. Its Soviet legacy of outdated and usually broken machinery, ramshackle transportation and mindless and needless bureaucracy make it almost as difficult to get into as out of – something you'll be looking to do from the minute you arrive.

Culture

Historically, Astana's culture was most closely affiliated with the beliefs and value system of the "Middle Horde" tribes that traditionally occupied the centre and northeast of the country. However, Soviet determination to expand the city led to an influx of people and a resulting swell of diverse influences from the tribes of the "Great Horde" of the south and the "Little Bitch Horde" of a small and particularly crappy bit of west. Not that the Soviets really gave a toss about tribal influences, having found a bit of the world so extra-terrestrial in its lack of life that they could set about eradicating whatever traces of existence are buried deep in the sand with 40 years of nuclear weapons testing. As a result, Kazakh culture tends to be a little confusing to outsiders – and even more confusing to anyone unlucky enough to live there. At the centre of this lack of certainty stands Astana, a town that has borne its name and capital city status for less time than Cher has had her current nose.

Attractions

Astana, which was known as Aqmola until the late 1990s, was an insignificant one-horse mining town until the Victory Day Feast of 1945 left it without the horse. It became the administrative centre for Soviet-controlled agricultural initiatives in the region following a particularly vodka-sodden game of "pin the tail on the donkey", which was organised for

Construction of skyscrapers combines conventional Western methods with more traditional local basket-weaving techniques

Khrushchev by his politburo. As a result, it's got all the appeal of any former Soviet satellite struggling to define itself without the threat of an engineered famine to motivate it.

With unreliable public transport your best bet is to brave the weather and get about the city on foot. This will be either very easy or very hard depending on whether you happen to be going in the same direction as the eyeball-searing winds blowing in off the steppes that day.

Eating and Drinking

Locating a nuclear testing site at the centre of the Virgin Lands agricultural development may have been one of Stalin's more perplexing decisions but it has given the Kazakhs a cuisine unlike any other in the world. It's generally recommended that you eat your main meal in the evenings in Astana. The horsemeat casserole may not taste any better, but at least you'll be able to see if any of your vegetables are giving off a radioactive glow.

Bangalore

In the heart of a country of incredible sensory richness lies a town with all the life-loving vibrancy of a chicken battery farm.

Country: India

Boredom Rating	★★★★
Likelihood of Fatal Visit	★★
Essential Packing	Telesales-worker union card
Most Likely Cause of Death	Falling telegraph pole

History

Nicknamed the "town of boiled beans" after the staple diet of most of the town's population until about ten years ago, Bangalore is the capital of the Karnataka state and has been a vital fortress town and administrative centre since the 16th century. The Indian government's awarding of numerous defence and telecommunications contracts to companies in the region led to a period of remarkable growth in the 1960s, until problems with the infrastructure became apparent, namely the fact that there was a limit to the number of plug adaptors you could run off a single socket.

Culture

As cultures go, India's is as rich, varied and diverse as they come. Tour the country and wherever you go you will be greeted by majestic vistas, unearthly smells and people as rich in generosity as they are in debt to the World Bank.

Except, that is, in Bangalore, a city whose soul has been clinically removed in the name of corporate efficiency. The arrival of the major banks, telecom companies and other evil super-villains in the city – drawn by the lure of first-rate graduates happy to sit for long hours in cubicles and be abused by Western consumers – has altered the city and its people irreparably. Everything about the host culture has

The natural scenery and parkland is carefully screened by advertising.

Bangalore city councillors have been active in zoning the city into nuisance-committing areas and non-nuisance committing areas.

been watered down, Westernised or otherwise screwed up. Family life is dominated by conversation in India, and families certainly do a lot of talking in Bangalore – just not to each other. This is because family members don't get to see each other. They're too busy explaining to you why the ATM just ate your card. To maintain family life in Bangalore, parents have to work split shifts on different time cycles. This means that someone is always home to make sure the kids get their introduction to telephone customer service homework in on time.

Attractions

Unless you're planning a guide to the world's largest call centres or have a fascination with theme bars so fake there are indigenous tribes deep in the Amazonian rainforests that wouldn't be taken in by them, Bangalore is a city to be avoided at all costs. The Government Museum is on Kasturba Gandhi Road and is worth spending a rupee on if you're a museum curator and want to feel good about the way you display your exhibits back home.

Eating and Drinking

The clash of cultures has resulted in some interesting recipes appearing on Bangalore's menus. Many of these "fusion" dishes work surprisingly well. Most, however, do not. In particular, the Dixie Fried Reclaimed Meat Thali with Kannada Chicken Bone Fries should be avoided by humans – or any other animal with fewer than six stomachs.

East Becomes West

The arrival of American firms in Bangalore in the 1980s has had an undeniable impact on local culture, with vegetarian restaurants gradually being replaced by Pizza Hut and Baskin-Robbins. And the city authorities' decision to host the Miss World contest in 1996 showed that they were out of touch not only with the rest of India, but probably with the rest of the world as well.

Bangkok

Bangkok is the doorway to a world of adventure for travellers looking for real experiences in the East. And it's a doorway that's about as inviting as the one on your nearest inner-city crack den.

Country: Thailand	
Boredom Rating	★
Likelihood of Fatal Visit	★★
Essential Packing	Table-tennis bat
Most Likely Cause of Death	Put-put accident

Street hoopla has never fallen out of favour with the games-loving Thai people.

History

Home of *Theravada* Buddhism and the only country in South East Asia not to be colonised by European aggressors, Thailand has cherished its proud past and contains some magnificent temples and well-preserved ruins of cities that date back some 3,000 years. Unfortunately, the chances are you're going to have to get there via Bangkok, a smutty joke of a city with stunning traffic jams, record-breaking levels of sleaze and carbon-monoxide poisoning that comes with a hint of jasmine.

A regime change in Thailand – then the kingdom of Siam – in 1932 brought to power an unusually moderate coalition who didn't see royalty as akin to the devil. The current Thai monarch His Majesty King Bhumibol Adulyadej and his wife Her Majesty Queen Sirikit retain both the approval and affection of the population, despite their largely ceremonial role. Something the British monarchy can only get nostalgic about. But while the country's relative stability is the envy of the Far East, Bangkok's transformation from elegant metropolis to GI playground during the '60s has made it the number one destination for sex tourists, heroin junkies and Americans with made-up war stories, and therefore somewhere to be avoided by everyone else.

Working in Bangkok

The biggest employer in Bangkok is the sex industry. New recruits will start out with an entrance-level job – and to be accepted you'll have to be pretty unfussy about which entrance it is that gets used, and all too frequently abused, as part of your job description. For those who are successful, the employment opportunities are as endless in variety as the sexually transmitted infections they're likely to catch as one of the legion of the city's rent-a-zombie escorts.

You can get around town cheaply and easily by monk bus. No need for a bus pass, simply find three onions.

Culture

One night in Bangkok may not make the world your oyster, but it'll certainly open your eyes to just how narrow your view of the planet was before you arrived. This is arguably the world's first 24-hour city, and buying and selling is done with the conviction that everything is for sale and everyone is a potential customer. This may be fantastic if you're a jaded hedonist come to town looking to satisfy your sickest cravings, but for just about everyone else the frequent reminders of just what dark desires the human mind is capable of nurturing may prove depressing in the extreme.

Attractions

If watching humans go sadly through the motions of getting pleasure from a ping-pong ball isn't your thing, you'll be delighted to know that they're not the only species performing under duress and probably under the influence in Bangkok. The Khao San Road is awash with animal attractions. Look for snake shows that have an older ringmaster unless you

want the unintentionally interactive element you'll get from an apprentice handler. Dancing-monkey recitals tend to be a safer bet, although watching the poor little buggers morosely shuffle around like teenagers at a Slipknot concert is likely to leave you with a heavy weight in your chest where your heart should be. The traffic, the traders, the smog and the oppressive skyscrapers can easily get to you after a few hours though. Head out onto the waterways if you want to get away from everything – everything that is except for aggressive boat people selling crappy resin elephants, overpriced Coca-Cola and Hello Kitty stationery sets.

Eating and Drinking

Eat on the street and who knows whether that black stuff on your chicken is aromatic spices or settling exhaust fumes – though with enough speed-laced whiskey inside you, you won't care either way. Smile and be polite with your waiter/chef and you may be able to reduce the amount you're being overcharged by as much as 10 percent.

Beijing

Ever since Marco Polo first struggled with a pair of chopsticks, the culture of China has fascinated the West. Sadly this infatuation is purely one-way.

Country: China	
Boredom Rating	★★★
Likelihood of Fatal Visit	★★
Essential Packing	Knife and fork
Most Likely Cause of Death	Having an opinion

History

What the rest of the world calls history, China might consider recent events. With an imperial lineage that dates back to 2200 BC and a justifiable claim for the original patent on just about everything ever invented of any use to mankind – not to mention a fair few things of no use to anyone – it is difficult to underestimate the impact that the Chinese have had on the development of Western civilisation. Europe's first contact with China came during the Ming Dynasty of the 16th century, which resulted in the

Children will adore honey glazed locusts on a stick – but try not to let them eat too many before dinner.

Even Beijing's most upmarket restaurants can suffer in comparison to most nations' public toilet facilities.

establishment of trading routes, none of which favoured the European powers. Finding themselves for once on the wrong end of a deal, the English set about redressing the balance. One series of Opium Wars and a dodgy fix-up of a peace treaty later the English took control of Hong Kong. The rest of Europe dived in for whatever territorial pickings it could get for itself and China set off on what would prove to be a 100-year roller-coaster ride that left a lot of people feeling a more than just nauseous.

Culture

China's transition from anarchic mess at the dawn of the 20th century to communist people's republic after World War II came at what many saw as being a heavy cost. But leaving aside the hundreds of thousands killed during the nation's "great leap forward", a term dreamt up by a man now recognised to be the father of modern political spin doctoring – not to mention the massacre of the student protesters in Tiananmen Square whose ideological devotion to their cause blinded them to the fact that they were taking on tanks – the greatest legacy of China's path from warlords to workers revolution is a code of manners and hierarchy of deference that would put Victorian England to

shame. Beijing is possibly the easiest city in the world in which to cause offence. And with a population of 13 million people – who all seem to know each other – and city boundaries that stretch some 50 miles from the centre, it's not a town where you want to make enemies. The safest way to avoid overstepping any social boundaries is to remove any element of the personal from your dealings with everyone. This is something that the residents of mainland China have been practising for years. Expect to see young lovers shaking hands as they say goodbye to each other and mothers reminding their tearful offspring to remember the teachings of Chairman Mao while they pack them off for their compulsory stints at military school. Take a leaf out of their book and deal with your own friends and family as if they are total strangers.

Attractions

Preparations for the 2008 Olympics have led to many of the seedier and greyer parts of Beijing being demolished, but you can still savour the flavour of the city's former greyness at the city zoo. The panda's special place in Chinese culture has afforded it star status within the grounds of this oppressive and terminally grim collection of terrified animals. While these pyjama-clad bears laze around in bamboo-shoot-stocked living rooms like contestants on a reality-TV show, the rest of the animals quiver and shiver in Guantanamo Bay-style cells, as badly psyched as Yvette Fielding on the *Most Haunted Hallowe'en Special*.

If your taste for the old and knackered extends even further, head for the Forbidden City. Despite the best efforts of a permanent restoration squad, a sadder and more decrepit selection of old buildings would be hard to find anywhere.

Eating and Drinking

The Western visitor who claims to know their way around a Chinese menu may be in for something of a shock here. The cuisine of China may be the most exported in the world, but it certainly gets improved in translation. Expect blank looks from your waiter when you ask for Peking Duck or Sweet and Sour Pork and prepare yourself for whatever gets brought in their place. Chicken feet are a popular dish and you can expect to be picking the knuckles out of your teeth for breakfast, lunch and dinner.

Don't be scared, these strange-looking horses are actually stuffed replicas.

Table Manners

Once again, it's remarkably easy to cause offence at the dinner table – though rarely for the reasons you might expect. Lifting your bowl to your mouth in order to facilitate such a rapid noodle transfer that half your sauce winds up on your chin is not considered impolite. In fact, as it allows the diner to devour food with the rapidity you'd associate with an American pre-teen eating French fries, it's actually considered a sign of great wisdom. Holding your chopsticks near the tip, however, is the height of poor manners and will be interpreted as a slight on your host. Looking on the bright side, this may at least result in you not being asked back.

Da Nang

Vietnam boasts a visa-application process complex enough to give Stephen Hawking a migraine and, in the dong, probably the most stupid, and certainly rudest sounding, currency in the known world.

Country: Vietnam	
Boredom Rating	★
Likelihood of Fatal Visit	★★★
Essential Packing	Magilite and surfboard
Most Likely Cause of Death	Avian flu

History

Like many a remarkable part of the world, Vietnam has a proud and culturally rich history that veered wildly off course the minute Europeans turned up on its doorstep and asked if it was OK to crash for the weekend. After successfully defending itself against assaults from China and Spain, Southern Vietnam succumbed to the French in 1867, causing a division that was ratified by the Geneva accords of 1954 when the French finally admitted that much as they liked Vietnam, they probably didn't need a whole one. With the communists in the north and the US-sponsored anti-communists in the south, the stage was soon set for the war that would introduce Agent Orange, the Green Berets and Black PJs to the world, and make the US realise that there was more to winning a war than just throwing vast numbers of tax dollars and young lives at it. Or at least it should have.

Culture

The West's understanding of the culture, people and history of Vietnam has largely come from the slew of movies churned out – sorry, lovingly crafted – by the Hollywood majors in the '70s and '80s. They depicted the country as a place where life was cheap and death lurked around every bombed-out street corner, where smiling farmers would feed you with one hand while signalling enemy troops with the other, and where girls too young to be out on their own talked the vile language of the streets and sold their bodies and souls nightly for the price of a beer. For once it seems Hollywood actually got it right. Turtle imagery is prevalent throughout the city's art and design and with good reason, for Da Nang is somewhere you'd only want to consider going with armour plating. The troops may have shipped out and the peasant farmers that once harboured troops of VC in their paddy fields now only harbour dreams of investing in another chicken next year, but Da Nang remains about as inviting to the traveller community as a freshly oiled mantrap.

Attractions

Da Nang is low on attractions unless you're into alleyways populated with fruit bats and two-foot-deep puddles. However, the city does serve as a major transport hub for anyone looking to get anywhere else in country. Travellers arriving in Da Nang by bus can expect to be greeted in the traditional way by the city's children – that is with a volley of rocks and dried cowshit.

Eating and Drinking

The food in Da Nang is great for anyone with a hardy stomach – a vast and varied range of spice goes into even the simplest of dishes. But there's a reason why your chef is taking such trouble to disguise what it is you're eating, and so diners are reminded that they should eat whatever they're presented with and not question what it is – they will invariably regret asking.

Modern homeopathic remedies owe a great deal to Viet Cong interrogation techniques.

Deshnok

Some people find the idea of cows being sacred pretty hard to get their heads around. But nearly everyone agrees that the whole idea of respecting animals has been taken several steps too far in the tiny village of Deshnok.

Country: India	
Boredom Rating	★★★
Likelihood of Fatal Visit	★★
Essential Packing	Hungry cat
Most Likely Cause of Death	Any one of several thousand rodent transmitted diseases.

History

Poverty, sweltering heat, 27 beggars for every traveller and the most dangerous electrical sockets in the world have not stopped India from becoming the essential destination for those looking to be different from the rest of the herd and establish their credentials as genuine travellers. (Though what it is that's so genuine about bumming around, smoking weed and getting dysentery while staying in accommodation modelled on the Black Hole of Calcutta.) Nevertheless, it's understandable why India has become the number one alternative travel spot for a whole generation of Western gappers – the incredibly diverse culture, the cute elephants and above all the fact that it's the only place on earth that you can get a decent cup of tea since England became a subsidiary of Starbucks PLC.

The city of Bikaner, once an important trading post on the great caravan trade route, now has a population of around half a million. Its most notable feature is its old city, surrounded by a high crenellated wall, which contains an impressive ancient fort. This is the place you will need to head if you are deranged enough to want to explore Deshnok, which lies some 20 miles down the road.

Culture

One of the central attractions for Westerners visiting India is having the chance to encounter religions based around fantastic creatures, bright colours and exciting and involved ceremonies – as opposed to standing around in chilly buildings mouthing the words to dreary hymns like they might have to do at home. Indeed, the array of religious choice available within one country can be bewildering to the visitor, and has allowed Western celebrities to pick'n'mix individual elements of different faiths, based largely, it would seem, on the advice of their personal trainers and colour consultants. Jainism, which bears many similarities to Buddhism, is one such belief system and is prevalent throughout the Gujarat region in northwest India. Jains believe that the universe is infinite and was not created by a deity – the kind of forward-looking thinking that can get you a court appearance in certain US states. Jains are strict vegetarians who maintain that all life is sacred and therefore go to extreme lengths to avoid harming any living thing. So far, so Madonna. What makes Jainism remarkable is just how this manifests itself in Deshnok's Karni Mata Temple.

Attractions

The clue to what awaits you is there on the base of entrance, carved in white marble – beautifully represented rats scamper for all eternity around the base of the entire structure. For the temple at Deshnok is devoted to rats. The main entrance to the temple is actually reminiscent of London's Marble Arch – the only difference being that here the rodents have taken residence on the pavement rather than a couple of feet below it. But beyond that, past an imposing pair of stone Asiatic lions, the fun really starts. Within a couple of shoeless steps you will be ankle deep in them, and with the rats having the right of way at all times, you'll need to make sure that the only little pink things that get damaged are your toes.

Bookings for Sunday
lunch remained
disappointingly low

Eating and Drinking

With their wholesome diet of fruit, oatmeal, grain, milk, coconut and sweetmeats, the rats actually eat better than a whole lot of the people in Deshnok. Visitors are encouraged to feed them – and then nibble on whatever the little buggers leave behind.

Sharing a dish with the rats is also said to bring great luck. However, Jainism is a faith that believes strongly in re-incarnation, and the question of whether the good luck will come in this life or the no-doubt-soon-to-be-experienced next one has never been satisfactorily answered.

What Have the Rats Ever Done For Us?

While catering for all the traditional human requirements of a place of worship – weddings, pilgrimages and jumble sales – the temple has been designed for the rats' convenience, with pre-drilled rat holes, fixed stone water dishes, a mortar-free inner shrine and a bronze mesh net to keep off birds of prey. Plans for a sacred exercise wheel are apparently underway. The rats themselves play a part in the running of the temple: water left over in their drinking pots is considered holy and is believed to have great healing powers. The central statue of Karni Mata is flanked by the Sapta Matrika, seven sinister mothers once thought to be the bringers of potentially fatal childhood diseases. So, the cholera had nothing to do with the rat urine in the baptism water then?

Kyoto

No-one can quite decide where the capital of Japan is, but Kyoto is certainly its cultural centre. And, as such, is the Japanese city you should avoid.

Country: Japan	
Boredom Rating	★★
Likelihood of Fatal Visit	★★
Essential Packing	Teabags
Most Likely Cause of Death	Faulty wiring on Karaoke machine

History

Home to the imperial court of Japan from the ninth until the 19th century, Kyoto was designed around the classic orderly grid pattern so beloved of the Chinese and Gap store layout designers, and its rise to prosperity led directly to the birth of the samurai. Needless to say, Kyoto saw a lot of trouble in the ensuing centuries, but by the start of the 20th century it had managed to establish itself as an industrial powerhouse with a well-educated and generally well-looked-after population. And what better way for Japan to mark its emergence as a major world power than by attacking China, signing up with the Nazis and launching a surprise attack on the US naval base at Pearl Harbour, an act of unforgivable savagery whose only redeeming feature was that it led indirectly to the end of Ben Affleck's movie career.

Culture

While Tokyo has established itself as the centre of Japanese business and commerce, and the seat of the throne has changed more times than Hiedi Fliess's sheets, Kyoto is now firmly established as the cultural heartbeat of the country. This may help to explain why, in stark contrast to Tokyo, the pace of life in Kyoto is fairly relaxed, with businessmen shunning the concept of the working lunch and regularly taking breaks of up to five minutes. And

after a breezy 14 hours in office cubicles that you'd struggle to swing a small earthworm in, the businessmen and women of Kyoto have one of the most beautiful cities in the world to kick back in, with ornate temples, beautiful gardens and colourful festivals. So why they're spending their hard-earned yen in ghastly Western-styled theme pubs singing bad karaoke is something of a mystery.

Attractions

It's hard to guess at what was on the minds of the architects of central Kyoto, but for their wives' sake you have to hope that they weren't compensating for something. Kyoto Station and the Kyoto Tower directly opposite are proof that size isn't everything – they are both undeniably vast and utterly gruesome. Go to the upper tier of the main station concourse and peer past the 130m-high tower to the north and you can just get a glimpse of the mellow skyline these two glass monstrosities have ruined forever.

Eating and Drinking

For all its drive to be more up to the minute, at least one ancient Japanese tradition is still rigorously observed in Kyoto – the ancient art of the geisha. For centuries the geisha of Kyoto have been practising their ancient art, and not surprisingly they're better at it than ever, succeeding in ripping off drunken office drones and bemused Westerners for the equivalent ticket price to a night at the Playboy Mansion in return for the world's most expensive cup of tea.

Unlike Tokyo, Kyoto has no ugly, sprawling bars

Manila

If we are to believe the insurance industry, that earthquakes, typhoons, floods and volcanic eruptions really are Acts of God, then he's very clearly got it in for the Philippines.

Country: Philippines	
Boredom Rating	★★★
Likelihood of Fatal Visit	★★★
Essential Packing	St. Christopher
Most Likely Cause of Death	Natural disaster/ botched rescue attempt

History

The Philippines came into existence in the 16th century – at least as far as the rest of the world was concerned – when they were happened upon by perennial explorer Ferdinand Magellan. He had just enough time to regret his latest world-beating achievement before his head kept its appointment with destiny in the form of a large rock wielded by a native with a different perspective on who should be writing the next chapter of the islands' history. Not surprisingly, the untimely demise of the Spanish envoy rather threw a spanner into the workings of their scheduled colonisation and it was 40 years before they could find anyone stupid enough to venture within spear-chucking distance of the island. And so it was that the Philippines were spared the combination of mineral exploitation and sadistic violence that characterised European imperialism at the time. The natives chose to spend this time not constructing defences against the inevitable Spanish return, but drinking coconut milk and working on their tans, so it was no great surprise when they succumbed to the onslaught of a somewhat better prepared armada in 1571.

Three hundred years of dodgy Spanish rule later the Americans decided it was time to free the islands from their oppressive rulers and give them the chance to determine their own future, provided of course that the future they chose was closely based on the American democratic system. US patronage led to the depressingly predictable rise of a total scumbag of a leader in Ferdinand Marcos whose most successful act as president was to extend the credit limit on his wife's AMEX, an economic decision that virtually bankrupted the people of the Philippines, but which led to a massive growth in the shoe industry worldwide.

Phillipine workers have nearly finished the task of putting Imelda Marcos' shopping away two decades after her husband was deposed.

Things are looking up in Manila. This riverside Marina development is now nearing completion

Culture

Since the days of Imelda's month-long shopping sprees, Manila has been a town where corruption is not only endemic but also as conspicuous as possible. After all, what fun is there to be had in ripping people off if you're not allowed to display the ill-gotten gains of your crookery? The institutions of the Philippines may be more corrupt than the Salem Witch Trials and designed as much with the benefit of the people in mind as the Palace of Versailles, but as least everybody's pretty open about it. In addition to as much high-level chicanery as you can shake a Swiss chequebook at, Manila also boasts some fantastic street-level crime, with some of the politest muggers you're ever likely to meet and kidnappers whose hostage-holding facilities often offer a beach view. Police presence on the streets of Manila is high, so if you should fall victim to extortion during your time there, do your best to keep quiet about it as involving local law enforcement will invariably end up costing you a good deal more.

Pushing the Envelope

Manila has of course given the world an envelope worthy of its name – A4, double-gummed and with re-enforced sides, it is generally considered the sturdiest envelope commercially available today, and arose from the demand for something that could be used to discreetly pass large consignments of cash to government officials prior to the awarding of commercial contracts within the city.

Attractions

Manila may have suffered from a lack of infrastructure investment, but that doesn't mean you can't have an exciting time there, particularly if you reach the almost inevitable conclusion that it's probably best to get out of the misery offered by its oppressive skyline and make for more rural islands. With what passes for a ferry in this part of the world sinking on average every three days or so, Manila can offer all the thrills of a trip to Disneyland with none of the sanctimonious family values. And with more than 5,000 islands in the Philippines uninhabited, there's still plenty for the island hopper to explore and discover for themselves – like just why it is that no one wants to live there.

Eating and Drinking

Manila offers a wide range of cuisine for the choosy traveller, unless of course you're unfortunate enough to find yourself there during a major religious festival – which is highly likely, given the level of religious devotion on show. Head to the rural outskirts of Manila's sprawl and you can expect the value systems of the locals you encounter to be a little different to those you'll have experienced in the neon-soaked downtown. Magellan's initial attempts to convert the pagans of the island to Christianity may have met with mixed success, but they've certainly taken hold now, albeit with a healthy dose of traditional savagery thrown in. The country grinds to a halt at Easter as herds of nutcases compete with each other to be the most worthy in flagellation and crucifixion ceremonies. Witness one of these halfwits getting nailed to a telegraph pole and you'll lose your appetite in no time.

Pyongyang

Statistically one of the safest places to exist on the planet. But give the Pentagon time and any kind of excuse and we'll see how long that lasts.

Country: North Korea	
Boredom Rating	★★★★
Likelihood of Fatal Visit	★
Essential Packing	Celebrity gossip magazine for Kim Jong-il
Most Likely Cause of Death	US pre-emptive nuclear strike

History

Formed in the first century AD by tribes looking not to be absorbed by the Chinese empire, Korea has been invaded and occupied by Japan, the US and the USSR in its time. And as if they didn't already have enough enemies, Koreans both sides of the border suddenly had an extra hostile neighbour after the country divided. North Korea embarked on a communist course after World War II under the watchful eye of Stalin's protégé Kim Il-Sung, subsequently entering history books as the world's most bombed region – during the Korean War. While communist rule in the north brought the usual round of disappearances in the middle of the night and enforced working holidays for periods of up to 25 years for dissidents, it also brought a marked improvement in the lives of those prepared to tow the line and worship at the altar of Kim. All of which has led it to a point of relative prosperity – by the standards of your average authoritarian socialist society at least – and given its leader, Kim Jong-il, a swagger on the world stage that even George W. seems reluctant to challenge.

Culture

Expect to endure months of application form filling and tedious vetting procedures on a par with getting a Blockbuster video card if you're considering applying for a visa to get into North Korea – and you'd be very foolish to try and get into the country without one. Once you've made it in, you can expect to enjoy all the freedoms enjoyed by the citizens themselves – none at all in other words. North Koreans are not permitted to travel around their own country without written permission, and even with that they'll struggle as there are no regularly scheduled domestic flights, few public buses and no more than a dozen bicycles. Succeed in getting hold of some form of transport and the lack of unsightly but admittedly useful road signs is likely to mean you'll soon be lost and arrested for stopping in a no-hanging-around-making-the-place-look-untidy zone.

Attractions

Despite its repressive atmosphere, Pyongyang is an attractive city with much to recommend it. A trip to see the two famous 150m fountains will usually be the highlight of any guided tour. Sadly, tours no longer include a visit to the world's largest treadmill and the teams of hapless workers who power them.

Eating and Drinking

Your tour guide will select a state-approved menu for you based on your background and country of residence. In all cases, pudding will be allowed only for those who complete their main course.

Land of the Beautiful

One of the most appealing things about Pyongyang is the people who live there. There are no street vendors, no unruly dogs, very few old people and a remarkable lack of pregnant women. This is because only those with the correct class background and appropriate level of charisma are allowed to live in this city. Their platform-heeled, Hollywood-fixated, absurdly quiffed leader exemplifies the level of visual appeal expected of those wishing to live here.

Sentinel Island

Surviving on the Sentinel Islands is a simple enough matter, providing you have a firm understanding of the age-old traditions practised by its indigenous tribes and can persuade them not to slit your throat on arrival.

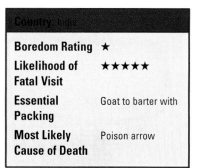

Country: India	
Boredom Rating	★
Likelihood of Fatal Visit	★★★★★
Essential Packing	Goat to barter with
Most Likely Cause of Death	Poison arrow

History

Part of India's remote Andaman and Nicobar Islands, Sentinel is thought to have been home to primitive indigenous tribes for as long as loincloths, big spears and fertility rituals have been around. Marco Polo was first to sign the Westerners' visitor's book, though he was diplomatic enough to refrain from using the name he had given it until his return home, at which time the entire region promptly became known as the land of the head-hunters. This being long before the appearance of aggressive recruitment consultants, the whole area was subsequently avoided by all but the most inept mariners. They were annexed by the British in 1869, but a filing error led to them being forgotten about until the Japanese occupied them during World War II. Rather than admit to any kind of administrative incompetence, the British Government were grateful to be able to release the territory into India's control in 1947, not that this made any noticeable difference to the natives living there.

Culture

While the majority of the 500 or so islands that make up the Andaman and Nicobar chain are characterised by one of two distinct cultural identities – primarily Negrito in the Andamans, and Autochthones in the Nicobars – the defining culture of the Sentinelese is that of *Pssoffnlefusalon*. Little is known about their way of life as any invitations made in the past to meet with the island's people has resulted in the RSVPs being returned on the end of a flaming arrow. Rescue teams sent in with relief supplies in the aftermath of the 2004 Tsunami found local tribesmen waiting on the beach, their spears raised and teeth bared in what seems to be the traditional greeting of the Sentinelese. The relief workers understandably beat a hasty retreat. Even helicopters dropping food parcels quickly came under assault from the same parcels being fired back at them from primitive catapults. We can only assume that rituals common throughout the rest of the Nicobars are also practised on Sentinel, the most notable of which is that of the living communing with the dead. Of course, this is not something any visitor to the region is likely to have to worry about – if you make it as far as Sentinel you'll be communing with the dead directly all too soon.

Eating and Drinking

The Sentinelese' remarkable ability to read signs in nature is what saved them from disaster in 2004. As legions of ants began heading for high ground, the 100-strong tribe figured all was not well and headed up the hill. Great news for the Sentinelese people, but pretty tough luck for the ants that gave them the nod and then found themselves on the menu that night in the absence of anything else to eat.

A rare shot of a Sentinel Island inhabitant taken over the shoulder of a fleeing photographer.

Seoul

Seoul is consider the most fun city in all of Korea, which tells you all you need to know about the region as a whole.

Country:	South Korea
Boredom Rating	★★★★
Likelihood of Fatal Visit	★★
Essential Packing	Hard hat
Most Likely Cause of Death	Tear-gas-induced seizure

Politically backward for most of the 20th century, the country's moves towards democracy were encouraged by the arrival of the Olympics bandwagon in 1988 and FIFA World Cup in 2002. These seemed to be working – in 1997 Korean workers finally earned themselves the right to be unemployed. And recent corporate scandals have confirmed that South Korea remains committed to aping the freedoms of the West in its business dealings. But thrill-seekers should be aware that Seoul is a safe city with a relatively low crime rate, so you're likely to be bored out of your brains unless you're lucky enough to get caught up in a large-scale civil disturbance.

History

The former capital of the Hermit Kingdom keeps a relatively low profile. Historic thumpings at the hands of the Mongols, Japanese and Russians, and the continued nuclear threat from the north has given the population an insular nature, and no discernible sense of humour.

Culture

Korean culture is based largely around hard work, with the average Korean working a staggering 108-hour week, not including an unpaid lunch hour, which Koreans traditionally work through as a token of gratitude to their employers. However, Sunday is treated very strictly as a day of rest and any Korean

The Koreans are known to eat dogs, but even worse, they often devour whole nursery rhymes. Here the three little pigs wish they'd gone for the brick instead of the bamboo.

Korea's answer to the Teletubbies (from left to right): La La, La La, La La and La La.

who attends his workplace for more than a few hours to prepare himself for the week ahead is frowned upon, unless of course he's cleared it in writing with management at least two working days beforehand.

Attractions

South Korea has a grand tradition of rioting, which frequently starts on one of the city's many university campuses before spilling out onto the surrounding streets and public squares, drawing in hordes of innocent bystanders and clueless tourists, who think they're part of Korea's equivalent of the Rio carnival. You're likely to end up part of the action whether you want to be or not, so it's best to be prepared. Gas masks can be found on the black market but can be prohibitively expensive, so pack a bandana and ski goggles and cross your fingers and hope that the police don't mistake you for a mugger – particularly as the standard-issue riot-police baton is usually taller than the man wielding it.

Eating and Drinking

No visit to Seoul is complete without sampling the strong pepper sausage the South Koreans call *ryuchi* – which is a shame as it's utterly vile. However, if you're looking to recreate the excitement of a tear-gas attack without any serious risk to life and limb this is just the ticket – the effects this sausage produces on those eating are in many ways similar, albeit on a slightly milder scale.

Speaking the Language

Korean is one of the most difficult of languages to learn, bearing more of a resemblance to Finnish than to either the Mandarin or Cantonese form of Chinese or to the Japanese tongue. However, despite its complexity, Korean is in many ways incredibly lacking in diversity or subtlety, and has a tendency towards the brutal. For example, there are a remarkable 19 words that mean the equivalent of "sadistic" in Korean, and a further 22 defining different shades of the word "masochistic". Yet there is no word in the Korean language for the term "fluffy". As a result of this it is a difficult language on the ear of the Western visitor. Even a friendly Korean greeting can sound like an order to dig your own grave and jump in it. You should not be dismayed by the apparent guttural harshness of the Korean tone – unless of course you are engaged in conversation with a member of the South Korean police force, in which case you probably heard right and should start digging right away unless you want things to get really nasty.

Ulaanbaatar

With enough space for Mariah Carey, her entire entourage and a good third of her inexplicably vast ego, Ulaanbaatar is the ultimate destination for those wanting to get away from everyone, and everything.

Country: Mongolia	
Boredom Rating	★★★★★
Likelihood of Fatal Visit	★★★
Essential Packing	Four-man tent
Most Likely Cause of Death	Runaway camel train

History

Despite a proud reputation for being hardy nomads, innovative farmers and heroic warriors, the Uighurs have been largely forgotten by history. The most likely cause of this is that vocalising their tribal name sounds a lot like violent retching, and can actually induce anti-peristalsis in the intestine and lead to extreme vomiting when done repeatedly. The term Mongol was first coined by the Chinese during the 7th century AD, to the intense relief of everyone but

Mongolia's top chefs prove they've spent years honing their skills, by preparing all the region's ingredients by hand.

the Uighurs, who'd got used to it by then, and was applied to anyone dwelling within Mongolia's ever-shifting boundaries thereafter, regardless of their tribal affiliations. This led to a lot of soul-searching for the newly christened Mongol hordes, not to mention numerous late-night arguments over the bonfire, and it was no surprise when it was decided to let the rest of the world know just who it was dealing with here in the 12th century. Genghis Khan's aggressive campaigning united the rival tribes and put Mongolia on the map. His mastery of horses, understanding of strategy and skewering of babies had his enemies running scared – or crawling scared, in the babies' case – and allowed his dynasty to form the largest empire the world has ever known. The death of Genghis' grandson Kublai left the Mongol Empire without an effective CEO, and shareholder discontent from the 14th century onwards saw its price plummet faster than Tony Blair's credibility, and it was happy to quietly retreat back within its original boundaries – the war-mongering nation's equivalent of moving back in with your parents. It gained effective independence from China in 1911 but retreating Russian White Army regiments forced it to turn off the PS2 and emerge complaining from its attic den to defend its fragile borders.

Culture

Ulaanbaatar is the capital of a country still in shock from the onslaught of Stalin's purges throughout the 1920s and '30s. If its people had any more taste for the idea of empire building before that, those days are now long gone. All it has asked of the world for as long as anyone can remember is to be left alone. Something that the world seems pretty much happy to do, at least until Shell find oil there. Boasting snow-capped mountains to the north and the Gobi Desert to the south, Ulaanbaatar is that most rare of things in Mongolia – a flat, relatively half-decent place where you can pitch a tent. That a city exists here at all is down to the resourcefulness of its

Ulaanbaatar's top tourist attractions include the Leaning Lamppost. It is overlooked here by the Ulaanbaatar Grand, the city's glitziest resort complex.

citizens and the laxity of its building-standards inspectors. The idea of building anything at all does not come naturally to the people of Mongolia, whose lifestyle has been nomadic throughout the region's history. And looking around at the Soviet-constructed high-rise housing blocks swaying gently in the breeze it's certainly easy to understand why the tent is so celebrated here.

Attractions

Anyone looking to "do absolutely nothing" while on holiday won't truly know the meaning of the expression until they've visited Ulaanbaatar. The chief activity for tourists is heading to Sukhbaatar Square at the city's alleged centre to organise a trip into the Gobi Desert, the only place on earth with even more nothing in it.

Eating and Drinking

As befits a nomadic society, the people of Ulaanbaatar feel that their lives are symbiotically related to those of animals. This is understandable given that there isn't a creature walking, flying, swimming or slithering in the region that you won't find a trace of in the digestive tracts of any of the locals. *Araq* is the local tipple. Made from fermented horse milk, it illustrates the high regard bestowed on the horse. Horses are revered in this society and allowed to live until old age before they are slaughtered and served for breakfast.

Go Go Gobi

Finding someone willing to take you on your own personalised desert adventure is easy enough in a town with as little to do as there is in Ulaanbaatar. And you won't need to worry about your driver getting drunk and swaying off the road, as there aren't any roads to speak of.

The city's skyline has led to it being nicknamed "the Manhattan of Mongolia" by absolutely no-one.

LET'S NOT GO TO...

Australasia

EXPECT TO HEAR AN AUSTRALIAN SAY:
"No worries"

MOST OBVIOUS LOW POINTS:
Nasty bugs, venomous snakes, cultural vacuum

SLIGHT COMPENSATIONS:
Barbies, tinnies and beachlife

OVERALL RATING: ★

★ ★ ★ ★ ★	**TOP BANANA**
★ ★ ★ ★	**WALTZING MATILDA**
★ ★ ★	**FAIR DINKUM**
★ ★	**DOWNER UNDER**
★	**XXXX**

Adamstown

A patriarchal island community with a terrible secret… Unfortunately, this is not a TV mini series, but real life on Pitcairn Island – and with no happy ending in sight, nor great location catering.

Country:	Pitcairn Island (in the South Pacific)
Boredom Rating	★★★★
Likelihood of Fatal Visit	★
Essential Packing	Complete Works of Andrea Dworkin
Most Likely Cause of Death	Declining a marriage proposal

History

The life of a sailor in the British Navy of the 18th century tends to get a pretty bad press. The reality was some way from the constant diet of rum, sodomy and the lash it's generally portrayed to be. In any case, if the sex scandals of more recent years are anything to go by, these three commodities are clearly essential to life in the British services. But even if the navy was a brutal and class-ridden regime, it was certainly no worse for those on board than for the families they left at home. It certainly afforded a welcome opportunity to get away from dreary weather, mundane cooking and interminable games of cricket. And when the men of HMS *Bounty* arrived in the Pacific and went ashore in Tahiti, they must truly have felt that they had landed in paradise. It is of no surprise that they were driven to mutiny when they were asked to leave a place where women wore the equivalent of a straw handkerchief to cover their entire body and where sexual favours to new arrivals was the customary greeting. What is more difficult to understand is that of all the places in the Pacific they could have picked as a refuge, they chose Pitcairn Island – an island that even the Spanish couldn't be bothered to claim for themselves when they discovered it.

Culture

Life proved to be no better for the mutineers on Pitcairn after they landed in 1789 than it is for their hapless descendants forced to live there now. By the end of the century only one of them was still alive. Their deaths were brought about by violence within the group, agents of the British Navy, and mainly through the realisation that breadfruit, the supposed

More tourists enjoying the multi-media displays at "The Adamstown Experience".

Downtown Adamstown; the crush for new building space is evident.

wonder food they had travelled halfway around the planet to harvest and now had a ship full of, was pretty much inedible. Seeing the mayhem all around him, John Adams put his criminal past behind him and discovered the Bible – quite literally, behind a pile of breadfruit on the *Bounty*. Central in establishing the quasi-British culture of Pitcairn, Adams became the island patriarch and did his best to convert the Polynesians who'd come along for the ride to Christianity. He got both a rock and a town named after him for his efforts. Since then the community has got along like any small village where everyone knows everyone else's name and your absence at church is noted on a Sunday. Namely, it's been carrying a guilty secret that has finally seen the light of day after decades of repression.

Attractions

With a population of 40, Adamstown has legitimate claim to being the smallest capital city on the planet. What's in absolutely no doubt is that there is sod all to do there. Perhaps not surprisingly, the lack of entertainment facilities on offer in Adamstown was not cited in the defence of the seven men charged with a range of sexual offences against the women and children of the island. Among the defendants was Steve Christian, Mayor of the Town, direct descendant of chief mutineer Fletcher Christian, and by all accounts no Mel Gibson. You can still check out the wreck of the ship commandeered by his ancestor – it sits at the bottom of Bounty Bay, no doubt alongside the bodies of those residents who were foolish enough to question just where it was in the town's charter that said orgies, statutory rape and paedophilia were tenets of the Seventh-day Adventist faith.

Eating and Drinking

Since there are no organised facilities for travellers, you'll have to rely on the generosity of the residents to cater to your needs. If you get the chance to watch them prepare the food you should; this way you can make sure that they don't slip a tranquilliser into your stew.

Burn Bounty Burn

Every year on January 23rd the island residents get together and burn an effigy of the *Bounty*. Whether this is done to celebrate their symbolic escape from English naval justice or to curse the ship that brought them to this godforsaken rock is a matter of some debate.

Brisbane

Brisbane has struggled to shake its reputation for being an overgrown village, combining as it does all the pollution, grime and ruined views of a small city with the kind of backward thinking you'd associate with a one-dunnie outback burgh where everyone shares a surname.

Country: Australia

Boredom Rating	★★★★★
Likelihood of Fatal Visit	★★★★★
Essential Packing	Rolled-up newspaper
Most Likely Cause of Death	Using an outside toilet

History

It's a sad fact that if Brisbane didn't exist, the British authorities would probably have had to invent it. As if being deported to Australia wasn't punishment enough, the penal authorities were forced to come up with somewhere to send those truly unrepentant dregs they'd forced on the continent who still failed to see the error of their ways. The tropical heat and unfriendly insect life offered by Queensland proved to be a perfect inner circle of convict Hell.

150 years later Brisbane has moved with the times, though, sadly, not all of them. However, this has proved to be a major attraction for many and the city's growth owes much to the legacy of local politico Joh Bjelke-Peterson, whose dazzling platform of anti-human rights, anti-conservation, anti-birth control and pro-corruption policies attracted new citizens by the trailer-park load.

Culture

Australians tend to revolve their lives around the beach. This may explain why everything in Brisbane seems a little off-centre, since its few beaches have all the appeal of a ploughed field after a thunderstorm.

Attractions

There are no state run tourist offices in Queensland, but head into one of the private travel offices and you'll be off on the trip of a lifetime to North Stradbroke Island or the Australian Woodshed Outback Experience in no time, even if you only went in to ask for directions to your hotel. Another not-to-be-missed event is the annual Australia Day Cockroach Race.

Eating and Drinking

Mud crabs or "muddies" are the local delicacy and can be up to 2 kilos in weight. And almost 100 grams of this will be actual crabmeat, the rest being shell, mud, grit and dried seagull droppings.

Wild Wildlife

Queensland boasts numerous species that are in many ways as odd as the state's *homo sapien* residents. Be on the look-out in particular for venomous cane toads (in bushes and trees), grey headed foxes (in the air, since these are essentially outsize bats) and redback spiders, that can generally think of nowhere better to eke out an existence than under your toilet seat.

Brisbane's architecture is a triumph of insect proofing over style.

Byron Bay

The centre of Australia's alternative lifestyle culture, Byron Bay has become a haven for yoga lovers, reiki devotees, aromatherapy disciples and every other kind of demented hippie the average traveller was heading to Australia in an attempt to avoid.

Country: Australia	
Boredom Rating	★★★
Likelihood of Fatal Visit	★★
Essential Packing	VW Camper van
Most Likely Cause of Death	Complications arising during colonic irrigation

Escape to the Cape

Head out to the cape for a look at the Cape Byron Lighthouse and you might be lucky enough to catch a glimpse of one of the region's few surviving whales – though you should also take care to avoid swarms of bloodsucking sandflies during months with a vowel in.

History

An unremarkable harbour named by Captain Cook after one of his close male friends, Byron Bay has made its name as a hippie haven since the 1970s. So it's something of a delight to note that long before tree-hugging became a recognised occupation, the principal industry of the town was whaling. The hunting of whales took off in Oz in the 1820s, and focussed on a particularly dumb and docile species the hunters christened the "southern right". Having depleted it's numbers to the point of extinction, the hunters were forced into switching the sights on their harpoons to the humpback when the southern right became subject to international protection in 1935. The construction of whaling stations in Queensland and New South Wales – including the Byron Bay Station – led to the slaughter of nearly 13 million humpbacks in the '50s and '60s, and a whole lot of tears before bedtime as a generation of young Australians were forced to finish their humpback casserole before they were allowed dessert.

Culture

Like a US premier with a murky history of alcoholism, drug use and draft-dodging, the town of Byron Bay is keen to avoid questions about its past and focus instead on telling everyone else how they should be living their lives now. The nerve centre of this liberal paradise is the Arts Factory Lodge, a hive of alternative activity with teepees for rooms, beanbags where the chairs should be, and some of the most wholesome vegetarian food you'll ever wish you hadn't ordered. Talent nights provide an opportunity for local singers, musicians and performance poets to strut their stuff and should be avoided at all costs.

Attractions

One of the few compensations for being forced to endure a culture frozen sometime in the 1970s is the spectacular coastline. Byron Bay's beaches are as beautiful as any on Earth. Sadly, you will probably not be welcome. The surfers and sunbathers take their respective disciplines very seriously and do not take kindly to the presence of anyone less beautiful than themselves clogging up their beach and hijacking their waves on childish boogie boards.

Eating and Drinking

Byron Bay has some great places to eat, and they're all prohibitively priced in the hope that the tourists will latch onto the fact that they really aren't welcome. After dinner why not head to the Carpark club. With a playlist consisting of hardcore techno you're likely to leave with a headache, but the club's management are to be applauded for attempting to drag the town out of the '70s and into the early '90s.

Darwin

Darwin may have given this city his name, but look closely at its residents and you'll see plenty of evidence to disprove his evolutionary theories.

Country: Australia	
Boredom Rating: ★★★★	
Likelihood of Fatal Visit	★★
Essential Packing	Knee-length boots
Most Likely Cause of Death	Rabid dingo bite

History

Australians share many things with the residents of Great Britain: a language; a huge chunk of shared DNA; a largely irrelevant monarchy, for the moment at least; and a grudging debt to the US for bailing it out of World War II. Possibly in an attempt to pay off this debt, the Australians got messed up in the Korean War, and even introduced conscription for Vietnam in 1964 – something not even the preferred lap dog of the US, the UK, did.

But any comparison between the two states breaks down when you start talking about size. Wherever you go in Australia you're still thousands of miles from where you want to be – even if where you want to be, unlikely as it may sound, is another part of Australia. Occupying over 7,600,000 square kilometres, and stretching more than 3,200km across in each direction, Australia could have been the country that the road movie was invented for, if the Yanks hadn't claimed it for themselves already. This is a shame since most of the roads are dreadful to drive on. Mad Max never had it this bad. Of particular concern are the juggernauts with multiple trailers that the Aussies refer to as "road trains". Catch sight of one of these monstrosities in your rear view mirror and you'll think Moby Dick has got himself a giant skateboard because he's convinced Ahab is hiding on your back seat. Coupled with the fender-wrecking potholes and colourful road-kill, these trucks of the Apocalypse will give you and your family all the fun of driving on a real railway track.

Culture

Unlike most of Australia there is evidence of some culture in Darwin. This probably has more to do with its proximity to Singapore than any inherent talents in the resident population. However, the current administration has pledged to develop some kind – any kind – of culture within the next 25 years and has put its money where its mouth is in hosting the largest Writer's Festival in the world. In the past this festival has been backed by many of the nation's successful authors, such as Peter Carey, and… err… the bloke who wrote *Schindler's Ark*.

Get involved in local activities, such as the Darwin Philosophical Discussion Group.

Though the pigmentation and scale are accurate, crocodiles in the wild rarely sit in an upright position.

Attractions

Darwin's location in the far north of Australia means monsoon time is anytime. Depending on the season, you'll be either uncomfortably hot and dehydrated or uncomfortably hot and flooded out of your discount-rate, ground-floor hotel room. But the swirling outback dust of the inland and the swirling golden sand of the windswept beaches both host some of the most remarkable creatures you're ever likely to want to avoid. Snakes to steer well clear of include the copperhead, brown, red-bellied black and Burberry check (this season and for a limited time only). Kakadu National Park has some of the ugliest animals you'll find anywhere in the world, and is only a drunken stroll away from Darwin city centre, in Australian terms (about 50 miles). Beach-lovers will be delighted to hear that shark attacks have dropped dramatically since the colonies of highly venomous box jellyfish took over the coastline.

Eating and Drinking

Eating in restaurants in Darwin is as cheap as it gets, proving once and for all the maxim that you get what you pay for. Like all Australians, the people of Darwin are sociable eaters who like nothing better than to combine barbecue food with bizarre entertainments. Try and get along to a Toad Race Barbie, but make sure you get your food before the race or you're liable to end up with whoever came in fourth.

Tin-Tacking

The most notable event in Darwin's cultural calendar is its Beer Can Regatta, held in August. As the competition may be entered only by skippers piloting vessels made of discarded tinnies, it at least puts the region's most abundant resource to some use.

Hobart

Q: What's the difference between Australia and a pot of yoghurt?

A: If you leave yoghurt for 200 years it will develop some kind of culture.

Country: Australia	
Boredom Rating	★★★
Likelihood of Fatal Visit	★★
Essential Packing	Industrial-strength sun block
Most Likely Cause of Death	Bad-mouthing the rugby/cricket team

History

Aborigines have lived in Australia since the last Ice Age, and did so in peace and stability until 1770, when Captain James Cook claimed the continent for the British, naming it New South Wales. Cook represented a new breed of explorer who sought to find holistic approaches to dealing with territories claimed on behalf of the Empire. Rather than stealing the land, digging for gold and enslaving the native population for sale overseas, the British instead stole the land, dug for gold, did their best to exterminate the native population and then dumped criminals from their home country in the space that created.

Australia's less-than-glamorous past as a bin for British societal dregs has led to countless jokes at its expense: Peter Cook was famously turned away from the country at passport control when in response to the question "Do you have a criminal record?" he asked if it was still compulsory.

Destination of the Sydney-Hobart yacht race, the harbour is crammed full of Australia's latest competition boats

But while it has been fighting to erase the stigma of its penal-colony past ever since convicts first arrived in 1787, the evidence of that history is all around. And nowhere is this more the case than in Hobart.

Culture

Hobart has two main building types: wheat-stoned, imposing buildings whose construction was overseen by foremen who carried bullwhips where today they'd carry a mug of tea and nasty sub-suburban pre-fabs that look unlikely to make it through a heavy rainstorm.

The heritage of the country's hard upbringing is a people for whom nothing is a problem. Unwelcoming terrain, killer crocs, big hairy spiders and a family-size hole in the ozone layer are just things that have to be dealt with, no worries. They even give their natural disasters cute names like Tracey.

This is also reflected in their attitude to all things cultural, where their expectations are universally low, as is evident from their soap operas. Australians can put up with the more pretentious stuff if they have to. If you've ever sat through a Mel Gibson movie, you'll know that they've had to put up with more than most.

Attractions

Tasmania provides a welcome change from the rest of the country's landscape, replacing outback wilderness with mountainous wilderness. Of particular note is Eaglehawk Neck on the Tasman Peninsula, which has some of the most evil-looking rock formations you'll ever have the displeasure of seeing. But wherever you go on the coast you'll be greeted by vertiginous cliffs that you'd be wise to stay well away from, particularly if you've already eaten your packed lunch, which for Australians comes in a handy plastic holder with six circular compartments.

Eating and Drinking

Hobart has several Italian, Thai and Indo-Chinese restaurants that serve excellent food, and many more traditional Australian bars and eateries that do not.

53

Port Moresby

Beautiful lagoons, open coastline, friendly people — just three of the things you'll find no trace of in this septic wound of a city.

Country: New Guinea

Boredom Rating	★★
Likelihood of Fatal Visit	★★★
Essential Packing	Self-assembly jet pack
Most Likely Cause of Death	Plate shifting

History

A collection of islands off the northeast coast of Australia, Papua New Guinea was discovered in the early 16th century by the Portuguese explorer Jorge de Meneses. With the kind of racial sensitivity that today would probably get him into court quicker than you can say "Silk 'n' Shine", he named it Isle of the Fuzzy Hairs.

It was left to its own devices for a few hundred years, until it became a bargaining chip in the early 20th century and then fell to the Japanese army during World War II. Finding little of any interest or value on the surface, they drilled 300 miles of tunnels through the imaginatively titled islands of New Britain and New Ireland, but to no avail.

The Discovery of Papua New Guinea

Historians disagree as to the actual date that New Guinea was discovered, but judging by the fact that its main harbour was named after the 18th explorer to land there, clearly no one was desperate to lay any claim to it.

The island was granted independence in 1975 and all was quiet until the 1980s, at which time the citizens of Bougainville Island had a look around the rest of the planet – at Chechnya, the brewing problem in the Balkans and ongoing issues in Britain, France and Spain... and decided that it was about time they were recognised as being separate and distinct from the people they'd been cohabiting with for the last few centuries. Arguments about the proceeds and environmental impact of copper mining led to the formation of a revolutionary army, military conflict, human rights abuses and a St. Valentine's Day Massacre that made Al Capone's attempt look distinctly amateurish by comparison. Not wanting to miss out on all the fun, Mother Nature chipped in with some death and destruction of her own, devastating the islands with drought, giant tsunamis, and the ongoing threat of tectonic plate shifting that has seen parts of the state sink faster than Kofi Annan's reputation.

Culture

You might think that the ongoing threat of natural disaster, persistent racial tensions and the undeveloped rawness of the land would combine to make Papua New Guinea a place with little to offer culturally and that it should be avoided at all costs. And you would be right to do so. It is advisable to stay out of both the mountainous rural areas, where travellers are vulnerable to attack from remnants of the rebel army, and out of urban areas, where high unemployment has led to a soaring city-crime rate. A provincial system of local government still struggling to find its feet has delivered all the confusion and bureaucracy you'd expect from a developed infrastructure with none of the actual benefits. And the use of more than 750 different languages means that even the most seasoned of travellers is likely to resort to using English, which is the equivalent of walking around wearing a t-shirt with "I'm a tourist carrying cash – want some?" daubed across it in fluorescent letters.

It is thought that many inhabitants of Port Moresby choose to build their homes on the water in an effort to get as far as possible from the land itself. Some houses have been built as far away as New Zealand.

Attractions

With its sprawling docks, dark smoky bars and architecture dominated by barbed wire and warning signs bearing German Shepherd portraits, Port Moresby has all the charm of an industrial abattoir, though sadly none of the cleanliness. And with a climate that veers from a still and sticky dry season to a wet season that takes the term "torrential" to new levels, the countryside has little to recommend it either, although you are likely to see some of the ugliest animals on the planet here – from the Goodfellow's tree kangaroo to the spiny anteater, and enough bats, rats and scarab beetles to strip your corpse of flesh to the bone in a couple of hours after you're gone.

Eating and Drinking

Scientists tell us that long after mankind has wiped itself out, the bugs will live on. Not surprisingly for a place that looks like a trial run for the Apocalypse, the bugs are doing rather well in Papua New Guinea. Don't worry too much about them getting in your food though, since in most Port Moresby restaurants the chances are they're already part of the recipe.

Rabbit Flat

Although Australia's most remote outback roadhouse is hardly a cool place to hang out, getting into it can be harder than blagging a table at The Ivy on a Friday night.

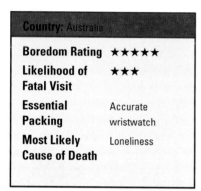

Country: Australia

Boredom Rating	★★★★★
Likelihood of Fatal Visit	★★★
Essential Packing	Accurate wristwatch
Most Likely Cause of Death	Loneliness

History

For years the Tanami Track was considered one of the most notorious routes across Australia's Northern Territory. Essentially a short cut linking the Red Centre to the Kimberley, it was used primarily by industrial vehicles servicing the region's mine facilities and mindless weekend adventurers looking to get into trouble in their newly purchased 4WDs so they had a story to bore their colleagues with on Monday morning. But since being upgraded to the giddy classification heights of dirt highway, the Tanami Track has become a popular route with travellers and tourists in search of the real Australia. Lured by the promise of the open road, dangerous wildlife and limited toilet facilities, morons the world over are tripping over their Timberland laces for the opportunity to hire themselves a dilapidated Land Rover, get lost, break down and be reduced to drinking their own urine before dying a lonely death miles from anywhere.

Culture

In such a challenging environment, travellers attempting the hazardous passage need to be extremely well prepared, which they generally are not, and foolhardy to the point of utter stupidity, which they generally are. Failing that, they will come to rely on the resourcefulness, generosity of spirit and commitment of the roadhouse owners along the way. This is something of a problem as Australian roadhouses seem to be run on the whole by anally retarded dickheads who appear to have learnt all there is to learn about being prissy and unhelpful from the English cousins they profess to despise. Whatever your requirements are, you can expect there to be a problem.

While even the laziest of businesses can expect to be open from Monday to Friday, Rabbit Flat Roadhouse is open from Friday to Monday. Confused? Well, you'll want to know all about the time zones then. South Australia is on the half hour. So, when it's noon in Melbourne, it's 11.30am in Adelaide but 10am over in Perth. Veer east and you'll go through two 45-minute time zones. All of this might be considered a minor irritant in everyday life, but when you're heading for Rabbit Flat as fast as the road corrugations will allow because you're on your last drop of diesel and have plans for the evening that don't involve fighting off rabid dingoes while you forage for nuts and berries, you'd better hope you make it before closing time.

Roadhouse Blues

It is worth bearing in mind that roadhouses tend to set their clocks to Perth time regardless of their actual time zone, which means that there'll be no danger of you missing *Neighbours*. If you're unlucky enough to make it to a fuel stop a couple of minutes late, you'll find that many of the proprietors will be happy to open up for you – and all of them will be more than happy to charge you 20 bucks for the privilege.

Rabbit Flat locals cycle out to witness an unprecedented traffic jam. It just doesn't get any more exciting than this.

Attractions

The Tanami Desert is home to numerous gold mines and, surprisingly, none of them is open to the public. Wolfe Creek Meteorite Crater could well be hard evidence that aliens landed on our planet, had a quick scout around Australia and then decided to continue their search for intelligent life elsewhere. Other than that, the best entertainment you can expect is to be had from keeping your vehicle out of sand drifts and praying that your spare tyre is in OK shape.

Eating and Drinking

Australian roadhouses aren't known for their cuisine, and Rabbit Flat is no exception. You'll be eating whatever you brought with you or you won't be eating at all. The water is on the brown side and deemed undrinkable, but there's nothing to actually stop you from doing so. In fact, the coloration and high presence of so many mineral elements means that a bowlful will pass for an organic soup once you've heated it up on one of the local bushfires.

Wellington

The huge success of *The Lord of the Rings* has put New Zealand on the map. But it's a remarkable location for lots of... well, several, other reasons.

Country:	New Zealand
Boredom Rating	★★★★
Likelihood of Fatal Visit	★
Essential Packing	Several good books. So, no Tolkien then
Most Likely Cause of Death	Crazed Tolkien fan

History

If the world is now a global village where North America is the police station, Europe is the library, Asia is the 24-7 and South America is the bar, where is the continent of Australasia? The back garden maybe? That would make Wellington a rock sat in a puddle in the back garden.

The country of New Zealand bears the distinction of being one of the few parts of the planet colonised by Europeans that wasn't just bled dry and turned into a battery farm for the slave trade. This may be because a typical native greeting in the 17th century tended to involve a long skewer, a fired-up barbie and, if you were lucky, a blow to the head. But it also says a lot about New Zealand that during the inevitable uprising against colonialism, Europe was for once more than happy to take a back seat and leave the Maoris and Pakehas to slug it out for land rights. This was partly because in terms of natural resources, New Zealand was bled dry long before the Europeans arrived, and partly down to the fact that, having circumnavigated the islands at the end of a very long voyage, Captain James Cook had a tendency to forget where they were. "... Turn left at Australia, no, sorry, right. Or was it left? One of the two. In any case, when you see Australia, it'll be on your left, sorry, right. New Guinea's on your left, anyway... "

Culture

The cultural vacuum of Australia clearly stretches as far as the city of Wellington. The most interesting cultural issue at present is the ongoing dispute with the Pentecostal Islands over who invented bungee jumping, a case that is being investigated by the International Directorate of Inane and Odd Things (IDIOT). The fact that any country could be so desperate to lay claim to inventing a sport that allows you to experience all the thrills of a plane crash minus the sick bag says it all.

But the islands have had some recent success. In both art and business, the country's current golden child is Peter Jackson, a hugely talented film director who is without doubt the most powerful New Zealander in Hollywood. But what the Lord giveth with one hand, he taketh away with the other: one look at Jackson's skipped-an-evolutionary-phase appearance and it's easy to see why he's made his living on that side of the camera. Still, his missing-link heritage makes him a perfect director for *King Kong*.

Attractions

Not surprisingly for a country where the sheep outnumber the people by a remarkable ten to one, shearing contests dominate the calendar and give the rugby-fixated New Zealanders the chance to remind both the sheep and themselves just who is in charge on the island. The Summer City Programme runs throughout January and February in Wellington and provides a showcase for artists, writers, performers

Shopping in Wellington

Visitors to Wellington should always check the use-by-date on cans of food they find in the supermarket, as several valuable antiques have been discovered in this way in recent years.

Despite New Zealand's pastoral reputation, there is a seemier side to the country. Here, Daisy dresses up for a Friday night in one of Wellington's new fetish bars.

and film-makers. The city authorities are hoping someone, anyone in fact, will take advantage of the programme one of these years.

Eating and Drinking

A place where a hamburger is deemed incomplete without a slice of beetroot and where yeast extract is a national obsession was never going to make it into the culinary Olympics. Still, there is food to be had in Wellington, and if you find the smiles on the faces of the island's number one species have made you too sentimental to try one of the woolly little darlings for dinner, seafood is readily available and guaranteed fresh from the harbour that morning. The lobsters are huge, and can be quite tough, so if you are having problems with your main course, notify your waiter and he will wrestle it back onto your plate and take it out to the kitchen to boil for a few more minutes.

EXPECT TO HEAR A EUROPEAN SAY:
"Hmmph"

MOST OBVIOUS LOW POINTS:
Snobbery, ethnic tensions, too many border crossings

SLIGHT COMPENSATIONS:
Varied cuisine, rich history, inept police force

OVERALL RATING:

★★★★★	**MUCHO BELLA**
★★★★	**JOLLY GOOD**
★★★	**COMME CI, COMME CA**
★★	**PAH!**
★	**ACHTUNG BABY**

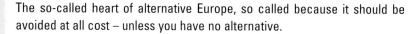

Amsterdam

The so-called heart of alternative Europe, so called because it should be avoided at all cost – unless you have no alternative.

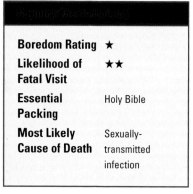

Country Investigation	
Boredom Rating	★
Likelihood of Fatal Visit	★★
Essential Packing	Holy Bible
Most Likely Cause of Death	Sexually-transmitted infection

History

Believe it or not, the Dutch have worked very hard to make Amsterdam what it is. Until the 12th century, it was an unstable morass of boggy marshland, and dykes and ditches were as essential in establishing it as stag weekends and Anne Francophiles are in keeping it going today. A Calvinist philosophy of hard work, decency and impractical footwear set the tone of the city from the 16th century onwards and Dutch sailors ruled the waves. Far too successful for far too long, the city was then forced to endure French occupation, British naval blockades, economic depression in the 1930s and Nazi invasion in 1940. After suffering more than most places during World War II, it was inevitable that the city would emerge a little unhinged, and in the 1960s Amsterdam emerged as the place to go in Europe if nowhere else would have you.

Culture

If you can put a label on it then it probably doesn't count as culture in Amsterdam, a place that's proud to be organised along anarchic lines and sees no contradiction in such an ambition. Town planners' attempts to eradicate car use in the city have led to the creation of the most tortuous routes from A to B since Theseus got lost walking his pet Minotaur, and have forced everyone in the city to adopt the bicycle as their primary means of transport. In a city that lays claim to being one of the most technologically advanced in the world, everyone is getting about on something any civilised person gave up using around the same time they got dental braces. "Road sharing" schemes have encouraged traffic and pedestrians to mingle – an idea about as inspired as Hillary Clinton asking Bill to drive the teenage babysitter home. Surprisingly, the scheme has been a remarkable success by its own terms. There has been no rise in casualties and traffic and pedestrians now move at a speed that's agreeable to everyone – about four miles per hour. This in turn has led to the evolution of cab drivers so objectionable they give even their Manhattan counterparts a run for their money.

Attractions

No visit to Amsterdam is complete without a pedalo boat trip around the *Grachtengordel* (canal network). If you thought getting around the city was confusing enough on foot, try it from a floating turd's point of view. Boats can be hired in one part of the city and returned in a number of others, which is just as well, as your chances of finding your point of departure are virtually zero unless you choose to simply sit stationary for half an hour. Factor getting lost into

Reality Check Special

The red light district is famous throughout the world for its up-front seediness, and a stroll along the Walletjes reveals a selection of sights grim enough to make even the most depraved of perverts feel like going home for a nice cup of tea and filling in an application form to join the clergy. The nearby Poo Museum neatly describes both the contents and the kind of experience you're likely to have should you be asinine enough to visit it.

how long you book your craft for, as boat-hire staff will be keen to hang onto your deposit and as a result will usually supply you with a map that's either impossible to read or easy enough to read but of another city – Manchester usually.

Eating and Drinking

Head into one of the city's many coffee bars and stock up on space brownies. They don't usually taste too good but they will at least make your stay seem as painless as possible.

The majority of Amsterdam's visitors come to see the Anne Frank museum, the canals and to visit the many art galleries.

You'd have to have a very good reason for going to Anglesey – but 60 seconds there is all the time it takes to realise that such a thing does not exist.

Boredom Rating	★★★★★
Likelihood of Fatal Visit:	★
Essential Packing	Compass and emergency rations
Most Likely Cause of Death	Frostbite

History

During the Roman occupation of the British Isles, Anglesey (which was then known as Mona for reasons of interest to virtually no one) was one of the last Celt strongholds and was controlled by druids. While the druids had some odd ideas about the nature of worship, they were ahead of many parts of the world with regard to sexual discrimination and equal opportunities. And so it was that that in their final epic battle with the Roman forces, a fearsome druid army of both men and women took to the shores of the Menai Straits, united in their purpose and bound together in their destiny, which as it turned out was to be slaughtered by their vastly superior Roman opponents.

Culture

Despite the Roman massacre, enough of the native population survived to keep the Celtic gene pool intact. Indeed, there are fearsome women to be seen to this day on the bustling street of the town centre. And while the Romans did their utmost to erase all traces of druid culture from the region, many elements of it survived and are still observed today – mistletoe at Christmas being one of the most famous. So, next time you get cornered by a dribbling moron clutching a sprig at the office Christmas party, you'll know you've got the Welsh to blame.

Unlike many parts of Wales, Anglesey remains a place where the people are proud of their culture and regularly parade in their national costume – a grisly collection of man-made fibres held together with absurdly outsized buttons. But with interest in traditional tailoring and regional heritage on the rise, traditional Welsh costume has been tipped as a hot look for next season – at least, it has been by the Welsh Textiles and Fabric Marketing Board.

Attractions

The island has long been considered agriculturally important, leading the mainland Welsh to give it the name *Mam Cymru*, or Mother of Wales – a name that manages to capture both the gratitude they felt for its role in providing a constant supply of food and their public embarrassment at being associated with somewhere so criminally uncool. If you're interested in agricultural methods, a student of Welsh barn architecture in the late 20th century, or just someone that likes the sort of weather that has even the ducks dreaming of the Maldives, Anglesey is for you.

Eating and Drinking

While there is a limited selection of restaurants on the island, pub landlords are happy to serve food and specialise in the national dish of Welsh Rarebit – that's cheese on toast to you and me – which can be served with or without salt and pepper.

Barcelona

Barcelona comes on like a drunken colleague at the office Christmas party – attractive at first glance, but quickly getting very scary, and you'll certainly regret getting involved in anything too serious the morning after.

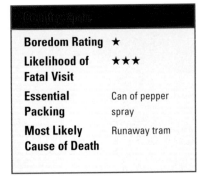

Country Guide

Boredom Rating	★
Likelihood of Fatal Visit	★★★
Essential Packing	Can of pepper spray
Most Likely Cause of Death	Runaway tram

History

To understand Barcelona, you must first understand the Catalan region of which Barcelona is arguably the most important city, and for that you need look no further than a history textbook. A legacy of petty vindictiveness, inappropriate over-familiarity and precocious sulking that only the Italians and Spanish could make such a big deal of for so many generations has led to the Catalans demanding that they be recognised as independent of Spain. This history gives the city a unique atmosphere that's in tune with its somewhat split identity. The people of Barcelona stroll the streets looking every bit as distracted as a supermodel in her first movie role, desperately trying to learn to walk and talk at the same time. Barcelona's colourful history, abstract architecture and easily bribed local officials have been attracting artists and armed thugs in equal measures for hundreds of years, and their work is evident in the many galleries and sculpture parks, and the constant siren soundtrack provided by the city's overworked ambulance crews.

Culture

Barcelona is dominated by the work of Antonio Gaudí, an avant-garde artist who lived and worked in the city until his death in 1926. One look at any of his buildings – the warped Gothic curves of the Manzana de Discordia, for instance – and you'll get an indication of why the city has always played such an important role in Spain's drug trade, both as an important distribution centre and a major market for consumption.

Other important works in the city that you might want to take in are: *La Pedrera* (*Casa Milà*), which comes over like Walt Disney as restyled by Charles Manson with a full-size *Star Wars* chess set on the roof; and La Sagrada Familia, an impressive cathedral built to atone for sin and appeal for God's mercy – which, like the hotel you'll probably find yourself staying in, is still under construction. Work is due for completion on the project as soon as management have agreed a back-to-work deal with the building workers union – making the situation exactly the same as with the hotel you're staying in.

Attractions

In a city so dominated by Gaudí's all-consuming if somewhat skewed vision, it's important to mention the work of Barcelona's other great artistic son, Joan Miró. His well-known sculpture *Dona I Ocell* (Woman and Bird) stands in the park that bears his name and has helped unite art critics and women's movements in their disgust at its phallic posturing.

Gaudí's Grisly End

Legend has it that Gaudí died when he stepped back to admire the completion of his latest creation…straight into the path of an oncoming tram. Whether or not the legend is true, the reality is that even if you are paying attention there's every chance that you'll be decapitated by one of the railcars that locals often refer to as *las muertos silencias* (the silent gliding death).

In addition to a wealth of artworks deemed important by whoever it is that makes these decisions, the city also hosts a number of important festivals throughout the summer, from *La Nit de Foc* (Fire Night) in June, and *Festes de la Merce* in September, which culminates in a *Correfoc* (Fire Race). Out of season visitors are also catered for by the residents of the many overcrowded slums just outside the city centre, who unwittingly host their own impromptu Fire Nights with the help of the poorly staffed housing department and perennially on-strike local emergency services.

Eating and Drinking

What Barcelona's restaurants may lack in terms of standard of preparation, quality of ingredients, courtesy of waiting staff and hygiene of chefs, they almost more than make up for with their excellent floorshows. Head up La Rambla, which runs northwest from the Old Harbour, and into the aging labyrinth known as the Ciutat Vella, and grab yourself a table on the street. This is the place to go for street entertainment, particularly if your idea of fun is watching two elderly women fighting in the street over an infant child. WWF has got nothing on watching two Spanish octogenarians go at it. Hair-pulling, biting, gouging and fish hooking are all on the menu and are accompanied by the kind of high-pitched caterwauling we haven't heard the like of since Guns 'n' Roses stopped touring. A great night out for the family, providing you eat before you leave the hotel and don't get too involved, as unlike their professional counterparts, these battling grannies will be all too keen to drag you into the action.

The troubles may be over, but with the right attitude and enough Guinness inside you there's nothing to stop you from creating a whole new set of troubles of your own.

Boredom Rating	★★★
Likelihood of Fatal Visit	★★
Essential Packing	Four-leaf clover
Most Likely Cause of Death	Saying the wrong thing to the wrong person

History

Historically a Celtic domain, the island of Ireland has struggled to resolve its independence issues ever since it came to the unwelcome attention of the Vikings in 795 AD. The English decided to chuck their oar in in 1169, and they became particularly uptight when an increasing Scottish presence in Ulster signalled the possibility of a Scottish alliance with the French. To this end they embarked on a number of military campaigns in an attempt to take control of the region, all of which were to prove highly successful for those working in the military dress uniform and naval wreath industries, but disastrous in terms of achieving their objectives. Changing tack, the English began to target the region as the focus of a series of ambitious colonisation programmes, the first of which was approved by Elizabeth I in 1571. These, too, proved disastrous, but the law of averages made it almost inevitable that sooner or later one barmy English scheme or other was likely to have some success. And so it proved in the early 17th century, when the establishment of a plantation in Ulster led to a large-scale migration of British Protestants to the region. All of which helped to create a society built on religious division, historical resentment and provocative marching and drum

Bars in Belfast range from the naffly themed to the frighteningly grim, and here you will be able to seek out some authentic craic. However, travellers would be well advised to avoid talking politics. Understanding the machinations of Irish history is a time-consuming and intricate business, and has yet to produce more than two people who agree entirely on any given issue. So dense with history, tradition and oxymorons are the underlying issues that even successive British Governments have ceased using them to score points off each other. So if the conversation moves in this direction you'd be well advised to subtly shift it onto other topics of local interest such as the spectacular multi-million pound robbery of the Northern Bank's Belfast headquarters in December 2004, widely believed to be the work of IRA foot soldiers with an abundance of time on their hands. Come to think of it, your best bet might be to keep your mouth shut at all times.

bashing that's caused almost as much widespread despair as Richard Gere's Irish accent in *The Jackal*, but considerably fewer laughs.

Culture

The principle of divide and rule worked all too well in Ulster, and while things seem peaceful in Belfast now, the atmosphere that a history of troubles has left is unlikely to be leaving anytime soon. Despite, or perhaps because of this, the people of Ireland are among the friendliest and most hospitable in Europe. Head for a pint in the ornate Crown Liquor Saloon and within minutes you are likely to be involved in

chirpy banter with, well, a bunch of American tourists trying to track their Irish ancestry in a bar that is seen as a tourist trap and universally avoided by Belfast residents.

Attractions

On the face of things, Belfast is indeed a city reborn. The only Irish city to be a part of the Industrial Revolution, its grand Portland stone public buildings contrast with the gleaming lines of the new Odyssey complex to stunning effect. But head west out of the city, towards the Fall Road and Shankill Road, and you'll find yourself in a terraced nightmare of grey concrete and political murals that will haunt every waking moment you remain in the city. With plenty

of bored ex-paramilitaries hanging about, it's a great place to find a cheap hit man.

Eating and Drinking

Ireland is, of course, famous for one drink. A combination of barley, hops, yeast and Irish Spring water – plus a supposed secret ingredient – are used to make Guinness, one of the most recognised beers on the planet. Rich in iron, this famous stout is seen by many as a meal in a glass, which given the standard of Belfast fare is no bad thing. Travellers are advised that their best bet as far as food goes is to stay in the pub and order bar snacks, resisting the urge to make obvious jokes about a lack of potatoes when ordering chips or crisps.

No country has done more to shape the face of modern Europe than Germany, which goes a long way to explaining the miserable state the continent as a whole is in.

Boredom Rating	★
Likelihood of Fatal Visit	★
Essential Packing	Orange-tinted sunglasses (proven to alleviate depression in all but the most chronic cases)
Most Likely Cause of Death	Collapsing wall

History

Even for a German city, Berlin has had a difficult past. Devastated in World War II, it was here that Hitler finally did the worlds of both international diplomacy and domestic house painting a favour by putting a bullet through his deranged brain. In the game of territorial gin rummy that followed, the Allied Forces, who were more than happy to carve up the rest of the country, were so desperate to avoid picking Berlin that the only way to come to any agreement on the city was to force each Western power to take a piece each and dump the worst bit on the Russians.

Long after the reunification of the Allied sectors, the city remained divided and Berlin became the focal point of the ideological war between capitalism and communism. The wall that the Russians erected on the night of August 12th, 1961, became a symbol of Soviet repression and split the city physically: a grey, bleak and oppressive concrete nightmare to the east, and a grey, bleak and oppressive concrete nightmare with Marlboro cigarettes and Coca-Cola to the west.

Culture

The collapse of the wall in 1989 has been attributed to the policies of *perestroika* (democratic reform) and *glasnost* (openness) introduced by Soviet Premier Gorbachev – but it would be only fair to say that the *kycment polski dratski* (cheap Polish cement) used in its original construction played a part. Today, almost all traces of the wall have gone and in its place stand residential units and amenity buildings designed sensitively to blend in seamlessly with the feel of the area. This has been almost too successful: in a recent

While the continued presence of street traders selling chunks of the original structure would imply there are enough raw materials knocking about to chuck it up again tomorrow, be warned that you will not be parting with cash for an actual hunk of the original. On a more positive note, this does at least mean that your souvenir should at least survive your journey home without crumbling to dust in your suitcase.

survey almost two-thirds of Berliners admitted that on the whole they preferred the wall and wondered if there was any chance of getting it back.

Where all of this leaves the culture of the city is frankly anyone's guess, but it clearly retains many of the characteristics of both sides of the former iron curtain. The city strives to project an image of anarchic decadence – strung-out performance poets and punk teens who look as though they sniffed some bad glue in 1979 and only woke up this morning litter the streets of Kreuzberg, Berlin's bohemian centre. However, in an unusual interpretation of the politics of anarchy, all alternative-lifestyle festivals, impromptu expressionist forum cabaret performances and even the civil disobedience and rioting is subsidised, orchestrated and run to a timetable with the same scary efficiency as the railway network. If Berlin is where Germans go to let their hair down, they're clearly repressing even more than we thought.

Attractions

Berlin has something for all the family, providing the family in question is the Addams family. Morbid doesn't begin to cover it. Start your tour with what's left of the Kaiser-Wilhelm-Gedachtniskirche, a once impressive church remodelled in 1943 by British bombers and now known as the "hollow tooth" in

recognition of its more open-plan feel. Then head out to the suburbs of Berlin. This will help you appreciate how lucky you are – however godforsaken the bit of the planet you call home may be, an hour in the suburbs of Berlin will make you pine for its beauty and warmth. Check out the former headquarters of the Stasi, the secret police force of the GDR – if you feel you can handle more grim grey buildings without exceeding your valium dosage – and round off your day with a trip to the Checkpoint Charlie museum to sample some of the kind of tub-thumping US imperialist propaganda you thought had disappeared when John Wayne stopped making movies.

Eating and Drinking

German cuisine at its best is generally considered to be simple and satisfying, and Berlin's restaurants tend to concentrate on the former of these virtues. Meat features heavily in everything, from Boulette (fried meat loaf) to Currywurst (spicy sausage with curried tomato sauce). German chefs are very thorough in their preparation and insist that the best cuts – from the sirloin, rib, fore shank and brisket – have all the fat and gristle trimmed from them. These vile off-cuts, an unwanted by-product in most kitchens, are then minced, spiced beyond recognition and made to create whatever German speciality you choose to indulge in.

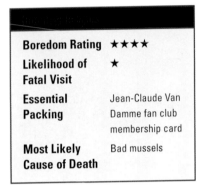

Brussels has a greater concentration of politicians, bureaucrats and lawyers than anywhere else on the planet. And if that doesn't put you off going, you probably deserve to spend the rest of your life there.

Boredom Rating	★★★★
Likelihood of Fatal Visit	★
Essential Packing	Jean-Claude Van Damme fan club membership card
Most Likely Cause of Death	Bad mussels

History

The area now known as Brussels has been populated since 2250 BC when a late Neolithic settlement sprang up in Schaerbeek. Soon man began to develop the ability to grow plants and domesticate wild animals, albeit with relatively little success. Early farming methods were unproductive, markets for produce were limited and over taxed by corrupt council officials, and consumers were frequently fobbed off with inferior goods as a result. And thus the seeds of the EU's Common Agricultural Policy were sown.

The town continued to grow and legend has it that St. Géry, bishop of Cambrai and Arras, built a chapel on one of the islands in the Senne (Zenne). Showing the kind of forward thinking that Brussels has become famous for, Géry selected a swamp for his site and it sadly sunk within a month of its completion. However,

St. Géry's vision and determination elevated him to the premier league of famous Belgians, alongside Edward de Smedt (the inventor of modern asphalt) and Jeanne Deckers (the singing nun whose number-one hit "Dominique" proved to the world that the Catholic church could still be down with it).

Culture

Brussels is dominated by public-sector buildings an average Joe like you won't be allowed into. However, the presence of NATO and the European Commission headquarters has led to associated industries springing up in response to the needs of the local politicos, and as a result Brussels is the perfect place to go if you're looking for high-quality paper-clip suppliers, all-night liquor stores or round-the-clock escort services.

Attractions

Belgians are famous for their modesty, and looking around, it's clear that they have a great deal to be modest about. Brussels has a variety of attractions, ranging from the disappointing to the underwhelming. The fact that its most well-known one is a small boy proudly urinating perhaps tells you all you need to know about this unremarkable city. Manneken Pis has been doing his thing with little regard for public health since the mid-14th century, and while you can't help feeling such a vulgarity would be ignored or avoided by the residents of any other civilised city, the Belgians take such pride in him that they dress him up in different costumes depending on the time of year.

Eating and Drinking

No visit to Brussels would be complete without an alfresco dining experience, which is unfortunate as Brussels suffers from some of the most wretched weather in Europe. Beg your waiter for an inside table and order *moules frites* – mussels and French fries. The mussels come in a bucket, which will be worth hanging onto until you're sure your digestive system has dealt with your offering to it.

Cardiff

Like a drunken nutter on the bus, the Welsh have been singing the praises of their capital city for more than 500 years. And the rest of the world is still politely staring out of the window, pretending not to hear.

Boredom Rating	★★★★
Likelihood of Fatal Visit	★
Essential Packing	Earplugs
Most Likely Cause of Death	Poorly constructed scrum

History

Like Scotland, Wales has a somewhat dysfunctional relationship with England, the country that neighbours it, helps define it and regularly humiliates it at any sport you'd care to mention. Attempts to establish itself as an independent state throughout history have been either doomed from the start – hardly surprising in the case of 13th-century Welsh champion Llywelyn the Last, whose name should have given him a clue – or horribly mistimed, as during the Industrial Revolution, when rampant nationalism was kept in check by even more rampant unpaid compulsory overtime.

Cardiff is at the centre of the struggle for a national identity and now houses the Welsh National Assembly, a building that looks like a bus shelter and was constructed to fool the people of Wales into thinking Westminster was giving them a say.

Culture

Despite a strong tradition of close harmony singing so relentless it has been classified a form of cruel and unusual punishment under the Geneva Convention, Wales has produced a number of important rock groups that have gone on to achieve international success. Whether or not they've enjoyed this success is another matter – Richey Edwards, lyricist and guitarist with the Manic Street Preachers, disappeared in 1995; Cardiff-born singer-songwriter Cerys Matthews abandoned her band Catatonia on the eve of their 2001 tour, citing anxiety and exhaustion as reasons for quitting; and Newport rock band Feeder lost drummer Jon Lee to suicide in 2002. Even more tragically, the Stereophonics have continued to write, record and tour throughout it all.

Attractions

Cardiff's Millennium Stadium is a state-of-the-art sports venue that would be an arena worthy of any spectacle. So it's something of a shame that it's used predominantly for games of rugby, as pointless a sport as it is possible to imagine.

Eating and Drinking

Despite its somewhat backward image, Cardiff has been able to secure investment from some high-profile sources. Hollywood actor John Malkovich has been an active partner at The Big Sleep Hotel since 2000. Despite its horrendous outward appearance, there are certainly far worse places to eat in Cardiff.

For many people, this endorsement of the city by a major Hollywood star has signalled that Cardiff does have more to offer the world than phlegm-clearing place names and absurd national dress. For most people though, it merely confirms that the always-eccentric Malkovich's idiosyncrasies have now blossomed into full-blown psychosis.

Copenhagen

When Shakespeare's greatest hero labels somewhere a prison, you know it's got to be worth avoiding.

Boredom Rating	★★
Likelihood of Fatal Visit	★
Essential Packing	Headache tablets
Most Likely Cause of Death	Supposing that you do not actually exist and then finding this to be precisely the case

The image that could be of anything. Possibly a shop, house, stables, theatre, still good in black and white, anyway...

History

Denmark's past is colourful and varied, in contrast to its monotonous and dreary present. It was a wild and troubled teenager, with Viking natives that tore all over the European neighbourhood and scandalised the residents with their taste for pillage, rape and pigtails for men. It settled into being the kind of career-focussed wage slave that's not above plots, poisoning and patricide to get ahead for four centuries after that, before a severe mid-life crisis led it into a series of wars that proved to be about as successful as Melanie Griffith's continued attempts to play under 50. After Nelson had trashed the capital and confiscated the keys to the Danish fleet, it did its best to settle into respectable retirement and was almost successful in it's attempts to stay out of both of the World Wars on the pretence that its back was playing up again. Now of advanced years, it has entered a contemplative phase in its history, and is probably best known for introducing the concept of Existentialism to the world. This philosophy attempts to describe our desire to make rational decisions despite existing in an irrational universe, and is divided into two main schools of thought. Existential Atheism supposes that life may be without inherent meaning, while Existential Theism suggests it might just have a meaning beyond human comprehension.

In contrast to Royal life in Denmark, Guards who work at the Palace are fairly stoic. Here a sentry mans his post whilst his cousin keeps watch...

"The Little Mermaid" is Copenhagen's most famous attraction and you'll certainly find her evocative of the rest of the city. Not that easy to get to and very disappointing when you get there, she stares mournfully into the water wishing she was somewhere else. You'll know how she feels.

All of which leads us very nicely to Copenhagen, a town that no one has ever quite managed to figure out the point of.

Culture

Central to all schools of Existentialism is the stress on concrete individual existence – man defines himself, his experiences and his environment in his own subjectivity. This is all well and good, but it does leave the Danish with no excuse for not redefining the environment of their capital, which is resolutely uninspiring throughout. Interminable blocks of identical six-storey buildings fill the featureless landscape and even the Latin Quarter is renowned for its neatness, good manners and early closing. It is no wonder the Danes have sought to escape from the tedium of their everyday existence in the fairytales of Hans Christian Andersen and the lager of Carlsberg.

While the rest of the world has "cool", Denmark has *hygge*, meaning cosy, or inside at least. A stroll down Stroget, the world's longest pedestrian mall, will convince you that there is nothing worth staying

outside for, if the constant rain and lack of natural light haven't already done so. The only drawback to installing yourself in a Copenhagen bar and counting down the hours till your departure is that you're likely to encounter a bunch of angst-ridden Danes wrestling with EU membership/what filling to have in their *smorrebord* dilemmas, and, like Hamlet, doing their best to opt out of the decision-making process altogether. While getting caught in a deep-and-meaningful with a Dane may seem agonising, it's probably preferable to encountering the one thing known to stop any conversation dead in its tracks – a live set by a similarly tortured Danish rock group.

Attractions

Christiana is a progressive community (where cars are banned) located in a former military camp. Have a stroll and take in the street entertainments, which include pointing and laughing at the residents' piercings and ordering organic food from a street vendor just to work out where the vegan pizza ends and the recycled cardboard tray begins.

Also worth checking out is the Tivoli Funfair – its genteel thrills make it perfect for three to four year olds and the clinically nervous. The Night Film Festival takes place in March and showcases anything up to 150 films that weren't good enough to be shown at Cannes.

Eating and Drinking

Danish pastries are renowned the world over, and some of the most mouth-watering you'll ever try are to be found in Copenhagen, where they are delivered fresh every day from neighbouring Sweden.

Edinburgh

The country that gave the world bagpipes, kilts and the inspiration for Mel Gibson's first attempt at rewriting history has a capital city as representative of its people as *Friends* is of the people of New York.

Boredom Rating	★★
Likelihood of Fatal Visit	★
Essential Packing	Audience participation indemnity card
Most Likely Cause of Death	Audience participation in a production of *Macbeth*

Since 1707, England and Scotland have formally been party to a common central government, but the reality has been an uneasy marriage, where the principles of give and take have allowed the Scottish to give all they can and the English to take all they want. But 1999 saw that most unusual of events – a government sticking to a pre-election pledge – and the implementation of the Labour government's characteristically ill-thought-out policy on devolution resulted in the formation of a Scottish parliament. Their first meeting was dogged by noisy traffic and icy winds blowing official papers around the Holyrood car park they'd convened in, so the first act of the new government was understandably to commission a new parliament building, blending the best traditions of Scottish architectural design with an English eye for detail in planning and logistics. As a result the people of Scotland have been left with an unfinished construction that looks like a game of Tetris as played by an educationally challenged orang-utan. And all for the bargain price of around a zillion (English) pounds – and counting.

History

For centuries the Scottish and English have shared an island, a language and a patronising contempt for the Welsh. Yet despite these commonalities and a long history of intermarriage against the fervent objections of in-laws on both sides, Scotland and England have always been two separate nations, each with its own distinctive culture, national

identity and catalogue of sporting underachievement. Not that you would know it from spending time in Edinburgh, a town so English in character that plans to extend the London Underground Northern Line to Princes Street are probably already underway. Historically this is understandable – the city has been sacked by the English on an almost annual basis since Celtic tribes first made the mistake of thinking that volcanic rock might be nice to bed down on for the night. Edinburgh's reputation for having one of the highest standards of living in Europe has led to further attempts by the English to colonise the area. The difference is that this time invaders come bearing not swords and bows, but merely a desperation to get away from the scuzziness of their their own capital city.

Culture

It scarcely seems possible, but during the month of August the streets fill with even more English people as the city hosts a series of diverse festivals that encompass military pomp, arty cinema and the very worst theatre imaginable. A twee town at the best of times, the combination of London media darlings, loud drama students and resentful Burgh dwellers, along with the ubiquitous Japanese Nikon bearers and even the occasional adventurous American, makes Edinburgh a place to be avoided at all costs during the summer. Which is pretty much the month of August wherever you go in Scotland.

Attractions

Arthur's Seat lies on the outskirts of the city, and considering the volume of crowds that flock up it you might think they were giving away free whisky at the top. Sadly this is not the case, and standing on top of Arthur's Seat is every bit as dull as standing at the bottom of it, plus a good deal colder. Many of Edinburgh's major tourist draws – the Castle, the Albert Memorial, the Royal Yacht *Britannia* – are, not surprisingly, monuments to English dominance of Scottish history. So, for a real flavour of Scotland you may want to visit Glasgow. Good luck with that.

Eating and Drinking

If you should be unfortunate enough to be stuck in Edinburgh during the festival, head to Oloroso, which is just off the main drag of Queen Street. The food may be overpriced and kind of fussy, but the spectacular roof terrace affords you the opportunity to hurl small projectiles at the annoying mime artists and manic leaflet pushers on the street below.

Faro

The country that gave its name to the Portuguese Man Of War – a creature so unpleasant that even the jellyfish family is keen to disown it – is everything you'd expect from such an association.

Boredom Rating	★★★
Likelihood of Fatal Visit	★★
Essential Packing	Tent and sleeping bags
Most Likely Cause of Death	Olive stone in trachea

History

Portugal's modern history has followed a familiarly depressing course through a rise in republicanism at the end of the 19th century, leading to a drive for democracy and the abolition of the monarchy in the early 20th century and culminating in a disastrous administration that was brought down by a military coup in 1926. However, the Portuguese have managed to make this formula for development their own by tempering it with their own national tendency for not really being too bothered about anything.

The dictator who became the beneficiary of Portugal's drive for democracy was able to hang onto power for a remarkable 42 years largely because the Portuguese people couldn't quite face the hassle of getting rid of him. And the length of his tenure aside, Antonio de Oliveira Salazar is at best a minor footnote in history – dissidents of the time were rarely intimidated by his genial interrogation style, the most brutal he ever got being to occasionally threaten to suspend their tennis-court privileges. Seen as something of an embarrassment to the community of international dictators, Salazar's death came not at the hands of an assassin but of a stroke, and when the military were finally ousted in 1974 the coup had the feel of a village fête – minus the shooting gallery.

Whatever time of year you go, you're bound to get caught up in one of the many festivals and fairs that can bring towns to standstill. And if you drive on the roads in Faro, you're equally likely to encounter one of the frequent auto pile-ups that have a similar effect but feature less sangria and no music. However, given the laissez-faire attitude that Portuguese bus and train drivers take to timetables, a car may be your only option for getting away from the construction site that is Faro for a few precious hours. Be warned that the characteristic "so-what" mentality is also evident in the behaviour of the average Portuguese driver, who will tend to see speed limits, lane restrictions and even your presence on the road in the first place as cramping his style.

Culture

Faro airport serves the Algarve and so most people's first view of the city is from a plane. And this is truly the best way to see the city. From a height of 30,000 feet or so the beaches and building sites blend together and the half-finished high-rise tourist developments exude a charm that's sadly lacking when they're encountered at ground level.

The greatest champion of the Algarve's charms was probably Lord Byron, who frequently hosted beach parties for his weird crowd at his mansion in Sintra, on the coast near the capital Lisbon. And the fact that he spent most of his adult life in an alcoholic stupor has certainly set the tone for the busloads of European tourists that descend on the coast each summer. Unfortunately, the fact that Byron was famously several doubloons short of a treasure chest

is reinforced by the culture on offer there. The Museo Municipal in Lagos is less than an hour's drive from Faro and bears all the treasures of Portuguese culture. Subsequently, it is an unimpressive, half-empty building beset by ongoing maintenance problems.

Attractions

Anywhere you go on the Algarve is an improvement on Faro, but of particular interest is the walled village of Evora, which houses a chapel constructed entirely from human remains allegedly constructed after a walkout by members of the grave-diggers union, who objected to a 15-minute reduction in their two-hour afternoon siesta.

Eating and Drinking

Faro has many fine restaurants, several of which are now nearing completion. In the meantime, diners who enjoy olives are in for a treat as wherever you decide to eat they will be produced between every course and will frequently make their way into every course too, dessert included. On a more positive note, Port-based Portuguese sangria is what a wine expert would describe as robust and anyone else would call lethal, so a couple of glasses of that and you should lose your sense of taste altogether. A restaurant of particular note is the Ruina in Albufeira, which adequately describes the state of both the décor and your stomach once you've sampled their Chicken Piri-Piri.

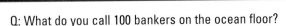

Q: What do you call 100 bankers on the ocean floor?

A: A good start. Unless they all work for the European Union, in which case it's an excellent start.

Country's name	
Boredom Rating	★★★
Likelihood of Fatal Visit	★
Essential Packing	Big idea/Un-patented invention/manuscript of first novel
Most Likely Cause of Death	Boardroom backstabbing

History

Cited by John F. Kennedy as the cradle of democracy in Germany and bombed to bits by the Allied Forces during World War II, Frankfurt rose from its own ashes in the late '40s to become the post-war economic dynamo that powered the nation's reconstruction. Its historical centre has now been rebuilt with an eye for detail you'd expect from the nation that gave the world the BMW 7 series. And while it has historically enjoyed a reputation for being one of the most liberal cities in all of Germany, this has more to do its primary focus – money and the making of it – rather than an inherent good nature in the people of the city, a quarter of whom aren't German. Principles and prejudice may exist in Frankfurt, but only if there's an angle for profit from them. Birthplace of the Deutschmark and launch pad of the Euro, it is a city where you are what you do, and where anyone who dares to attempt an alternative lifestyle is swiftly awarded a generous grant in order to heave them on board with the establishment. Social engineering on this scale has meant that Frankfurt's unemployment rate is consistently the lowest in the country. It has also filled its numerous galleries with the most self-indulgent and pointless so-called works of art you're ever likely to be bored to tears by outside of a Tracey Emin exhibition.

Culture

The grey, grim high-rise austerity of the north and west of the city may be in stark contrast to the grey, grim low-rise austerity of the south, but make no

mistake that it is in the financial hub of the north that you'll find the city's heartbeat. This may explain why time in Frankfurt is about as enjoyable as spending an afternoon discussing tax liability with your accountant. In addition to artworks that look like the average IKEA-shopper's abandoned attempt to self assemble a Poncigg computer desk without instructions, the city is also immensely proud of its musical heritage. As well as giving the world secular choral music that could stop an army of invading aliens in its tracks, Frankfurt invented Kraftwerk, music produced not merely by machines but also for machines judging by the sound of it.

Attractions

Frankfurt has long been one of the most important convention centres in all of Europe, if not the world. Every year between March and October the city is flooded by delegates and experts in their fields, keen to address the key questions that are perplexing their respective industries. Questions such as "Why do we have to have our convention in Frankfurt again this year?" "What are the little ante rooms in all the bars used for?" and "What is it that Germans have against their own pubic hair? Or against wearing a towel or trunks in the sauna for that matter?"

Eating and Drinking

Once you've had enough of the prosperous north, head across the Untermainbrucke and bag yourself an outside table in Sachsenhausen. The food is every bit as appetising as any you'll find in Germany – so, not very then. However, you will have a ringside seat for the procession of expense-account conventioneers unused to the combination of vast quantities of strong liquor and a major river that has no barrier to keep them from falling headlong into it.

Frankfurt – The Big Apple Strudel

Since its restoration, and given its vital role in international business and finance, Frankfurt has been in the market for a catchy nickname for as long as anyone can remember. Its current attempt to promote itself as "Mainhattan", based both on the river that it is built on and its self-professed similarities to the heart of NYC, has been about as successful as the introduction of a smoking gallery on the Hindenburg.

Don't be taken in by the pictures you've seen. It's just a model.

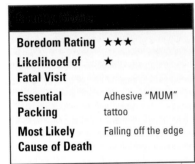

Boredom Rating	★★★	
Likelihood of Fatal Visit	★	
Essential Packing	Adhesive "MUM" tattoo	
Most Likely Cause of Death	Falling off the edge	

History

Captured by the Anglo-Dutch fleet during the War of the Spanish Succession in 1704, the Rock of Gibraltar was surrendered to the British in 1713 by the Spanish, who have been asking for it back ever since. However, British authorities remain unlikely to surrender the Rock, knowing its strategic value as a naval base and, more importantly, relishing the fact that British control of it pisses off the Spanish no end. And while the border was closed between 1967 and 1985, this did not impede the Gibraltarians' ability to transform the Rock from a quaint little corner of Spain reaching out towards the tip of North Africa to a hellish dump where Brits could feel they were still back in their depressing little suburbs if it wasn't for all the sunshine.

Culture

You might expect the culture of the Rock, which occupies a spot on the southeastern tip of the Iberian Peninsula, to be a blend of Spanish, British and Moroccan, with all the added colour that comes of being a vital port that serves as a gateway between the Mediterranean Sea and Atlantic Ocean. But you would be wrong. Culture comes in two main forms on the Rock: old episodes of *Only Fools and Horses* viewed on poor-quality widescreen TVs with the volume maxed out and endless English Premiership Football matches viewed on poor-quality projection screens with no sound at all.

Attractions

Camping is not allowed on the Rock, and hotels are expensive and lacking in luxuries such as TVs, showers and beds. But should you decide against your better judgement to stay, a cable car to the top of the Rock is one way – if not the only way – to pass the time. Once you've enjoyed the view of 1,000 places in southern Spain you'd have been far better off going to, head to the nature reserve for a chance to meet the Rock's most famous residents, who are also its most intelligent source of conversation, unless you're lucky enough to get a housemaid that speaks some English. Like the sailors on the Rock on shore leave, the Barbary Apes may seem friendly at first, but they can become quickly aggressive in packs, so you may want to observe them from a distance. You can tell the two species apart by the long grey body hair, which the apes have, and the pronounced swollen red markings that appear around the anal cavity, which the apes do not have.

Welcome to the Rock

An imposing and impressive sight when viewed on the horizon, Gibraltar becomes less and less appealing the closer you get to it. And if getting close to it makes you uncertain about whether or not you want to proceed, the welcome you'll get on arrival should leave you in no doubt that even the worst parts of the Costa del Sol have more to offer than this godforsaken oddity. Once you've managed to get past some of the most hostile border guards known to man since Checkpoint Charlie closed down, you'll be offered an approach to town across an operational aircraft runway. Since it's a mile from the border crossing to any available cover, you're advised to travel light and pack training shoes.

For holidaymakers, Gibraltar is as welcoming as the giant shark fin on the horizon it so closely resembles.

Eating and Drinking

Food available in the Rock's many English themed style pubs is the traditional fare served as an accompaniment to a quiet night's binge drinking, so the hungry traveller can look forward to dining on prawn cocktail, roast chicken, cheese and onion, salt and vinegar or ready salted.

Glasgow

Like Sherlock Holmes and Professor Moriarty or Pepsi and Coke, Glasgow and Edinburgh are defined by their eternal quest to better their nemesis. Which is fine with most Glaswegians, as they are always up for a fight.

Guide to Glasgow	
Boredom Rating	★★
Likelihood of Fatal Visit	★★★
Essential Packing	Knuckledusters
Most Likely Cause of Death	Not being Glaswegian

History

The city of Glasgow dates back to 500 AD. Not that you'd know it from the architecture, which is a grim blend of '60s concrete development, Industrial Revolution relics and sprawling self-assembly warehouse complexes that look as if they've been shipped in from Mordor. Tobacco importing, munitions manufacturing, shipbuilding and textiles made the city one of the most vibrant centres of production in Europe during the 18th and 19th centuries, while tobacco consumption, tenement housing, cholera outbreaks and whisky-fuelled brawling kept the population at a manageable level. But recession in the late '70s has transformed it from a city that's working class and proud of it into an urban wasteland whose chief exports are now broken dreams, aggressive drunks and bag ladies who've pissed themselves. Named the UK's City of Architecture and Design in 1999 – presumably because of the amount of potential business it will generate for Architects and Designers as soon as someone is sensible enough to propose the demolition of every building standing there at the moment – it remains a destination that can justifiably inspire terror in even the most seasoned of travellers.

The people of Glasgow are interested in you being in a peaceful queue.

Culture

Unlike its mortal enemy and local rival, Edinburgh, Glasgow is a place where it's possible to sample Scottish culture beyond its more genteel shortbread forms. While the tenement blocks of Edinburgh are now the sole preserve of web designers and trust-fund students looking for some freedom from mater and pater down south, Glasgow's squalid blocks are still the domain of the smelly and impoverished they were designed for. The most intimidating of these is the Gorbals Estate in the East End of the city, a concrete jungle where the threat of violence is as prevalent as the stench of extra-strength lager. If you're lucky enough to avoid the attentions of the local dealers and destitutes here, there's still a good chance you'll be downed by the most tooled-up police in the UK – who've justifiably assumed you're a visiting crime lord because you're wearing a coat.

Attractions

Probably the best collection of art in the city is on show at the Kelvingrove Gallery and Museum. Works by Botticelli, Van Gogh, Rembrandt, Picasso and Monet are among those you won't be able to see since the building is currently closed – supposedly for refurbishment. The gallery administrators have strenuously denied that the former director was forced to sell off the bulk of their collection to keep up their hefty protection payments. Tenement House is a National Trust preserved apartment of the type where Glasgow's lower classes – who represent about 98 percent of the population – used to live before they were all evicted and took up permanent residence on park benches and night buses.

Eating and Drinking

Glasgow's cuisine tells you everything you need to know about the changing face of the British diet in modern times. The working population spent most of the 18th and 19th centuries – not to mention the first half of the 20th century, at least until rationing was over – in a state of permanent malnutrition. Now the average Glaswegian, if such a thing exists, tends to sport a waistline that wouldn't look out of place in a Jerry Springer audience. Crucial to the preparation of anything you eat in Glasgow is the deep-fat fryer. Burgers, pizza and – most famously – Mars Bars are all made even more unhealthy by this means, but Glaswegian chefs are always looking for new things to fatten up, and so don't be surprised to find muesli,

salad and fruit sorbet all getting the Glasgow treatment in whichever establishment you're unlucky enough to end up staying.

National Story

The Scots continue to follow football with a rare passion, despite the fact that their national side is now below the Samoan Women's Volleyball team in the FIFA rankings. And there's nothing to compare to the atmosphere of an old firm derby between (Protestant) Rangers and (Catholic) Celtic. After the game you can look forward to seeing – or maybe even getting involved in – violent clashes between fans fired up by both mutual hatred and religious intolerance.

Despite fierce opposition from just about everyone who lives there (as well as everyone who doesn't), the Russians have managed to give the beleaguered people of Grozny one thing that's truly state-of the-art: Chechens now enjoy the benefits of an election-rigging machine that's the envy of the world.

Boredom Rating	N/A
Likelihood of Fatal Visit	★★★★★
Essential Packing	White flag
Most Likely Cause of Death	Coming out from under the table

History

Chechnya lies at the point on earth where Asia and Europe bleed together, all too often literally, and throughout history it has proved to be a melting pot with far too many chefs desperate to dominate the broth's recipe with their own signature ingredients. The Chechens were first recognised as being a distinct people in the 17th century, mainly because

With almost as many checkpoints as Baghdad, Grozny has become as grid locked as London in the last ten years. And while drivers in Grozny aren't yet charged for the privilege of sitting around waiting to occasionally shuffle forwards a few metres, the authorities have introduced a series of measures known as normalisation, one of which has been to keep the checkpoints open after curfew. Whilst this may have made life easier for guerrilla fighters working within the capital, it has at least forced them into working unsociable hours.

they were the only people in central Asia to put up much of a fight against the expanding Russian Empire, a fight that they are continuing to lose to this day. Not terribly taken with becoming part of the Chechen-Ingush Autonomous Soviet Socialist Republic in 1934, the region not surprisingly topped the tables for deportation throughout Stalin's happy reign. And it has continued to fight for genuine independence against a Russian Army that loses more troops to malnutrition than to enemy fire.

Culture

Officially recognised as one of the three most dangerous places on the planet, Chechnya's culture is, by necessity, of the duck-and-cover variety. Home to one of Russia's largest crime families, besieged by Putin's troops and policed by a special unit called the Omon, who are regularly nominated in the Best Use of a Blunt Instrument category at the Secret Policeman's Annual Awards, it boasts a selection of ravaged museums and collapsed galleries that have to be found down bombed-out streets to be believed. Blown to bits during the war of 1994–6, Grozny Museum does benefit at least from a central location, so despite the absence of any exhibits it enjoys a considerable footfall from residents and tourists looking to get out of the rain, and more frequently still, the gunfire.

Attractions

Zachistki clean-up operations by Russian forces have ensured that the people here spend as little time out of their homes as possible. Those that are brave enough to actually venture out are probably not the people to ask for directions unless you're a mystery shopper for a travel-insurance firm. On a more positive note, men so ugly they never thought they'd find love, true or otherwise, will be delighted to learn

The military presence in Grozny has given its citizens a renewed sense of hope.

that an introduction to a single woman in Chechnya is almost always followed by a marriage proposal.

Eating and Drinking

Chechnya boasts some fine restaurants that serve traditional Georgian dishes. So, with kidnapping and political assassination always on the menu in Grozny, you'll want to stay away from these dangerous-situation magnets unless you're looking to extend your stay indefinitely or you like the idea of picking pieces of politico brain out of your *borscht*.

Helsinki

Helsinki combines the old-world charm of a McDonalds drive-thru with the dynamic pace of a retirement home bridge night.

Country: Finland	
Boredom Rating	★★★★★
Likelihood of Fatal Visit	★★★
Essential Packing	Prozac
Most Likely Cause of Death	Assisted suicide

History

Founded in 1550 by Swedish King Gustav Vasa, Helsinki is perhaps most famous for being the sixth oldest town in Finland. Desperate for a trading town to rival Tallin, the present-day capital of Estonia, the misguidedly optimistic monarch established a royal decree forcing traders from Ekenäs and a few other towns to head off and set up shop in the newly founded settlement, known then as Helsingfors (literally, godforsaken wasteland of rock). The citizens of Helsinki have retained an understandably suspicious attitude towards royalty ever since. For more than 200 years Helsinki remained a backwater, one-horse market town on a windy, rocky peninsula. Then, sadly, the horse died, and things started to get

really dull. However, a devastating blaze ripped through the town in 1808, which certainly livened things up – particularly as the complexity of the developing Finnish language meant the Finns had yet to come up with words meaning "Fire", "Get the hell out" or "Is it just me or is something burning in here?" Still, the inferno provided an impetus to rebuild Helsinki in a manner befitting a capital. Why then the Finns chose to come up with a design concept that maintained a rigid focus on keeping the Herring Market at the centre of everything is perhaps something of a mystery. However, the planning authorities' commitment to keeping Helsinki free of high-rise buildings has at least helped to reduce the number of high-profile suicides in the city centre. Unfortunately, it seems to have merely pushed the problem into the provinces and today Finland has the highest adult male suicide rate in Europe, with ambitions to one day top the world league table.

Culture

Finland poses a number of challenging questions for the cultural analyst. Questions such as "Does Finland have a culture at all? And if so, where the hell can I find it?" A short stroll through downtown Helsinki, and you'll find yourself all too quickly in uptown Helsinki, and then before you know it, rural Helsinki – though you'll be hard pushed to spot any real difference. Turn around and head back to the tram terminus that passes for a city and this time remain stationary. You'll quickly see the incredible diversity of cultures and influences competing for your attention – though as competitions go it seems to have been won by default as the home team don't seem to have turned up. Italian-style pizzerias, Stateside-style burger bars and Irish themed bars serving real Irish Guinness (brewed under licence in Vantaa) present a real variety of choice for the tourist looking for somewhere fun to spend the evening. Feel safe in the knowledge that once you're indoors, all Finnish establishments look and feel the same – that is, like a mausoleum with styling by IKEA.

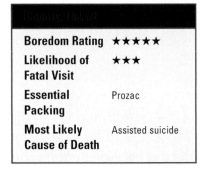

Just like with Eros in London's Piccadilly Circus or the central traffic island of New York's Times Square, the youth of the city have made one of the Helsinki's landmarks their own. In this case it's the Stockmann sign, advertising the department store, famous throughout Finland for it extensive drapery department. A place for the teens to meet, hang out and wait for something – anything – to happen.

Attractions

Helsinki has plenty to offer any visitor, providing that visitor is a seagull. The options are more limited for human beings, unless you have an unnatural fascination with herrings. The Herring Festival is the highlight of Helsinki's social calendar, and runs in the *kauppatori* (market square) throughout October. While few visitors to the city would describe it as being an unmissable event, most would say it is certainly unavoidable.

Other than that, your options are limited to staring out to the sea that surrounds the peninsula on which the city is built and contemplating the futility of your existence (a popular pastime throughout Finland, and indeed, Scandinavia as a whole) or heading out of town and exploring the imposing forest that surrounds you on every side. Be aware, though, that due to the country's northern latitude, daylight hours can be limited – in July and August you can expect a mere six hours daylight, but this is considerably less during the winter months (September to June).

Eating and Drinking

Many travellers who've never experienced the best in Finnish cuisine assume that it is based predominantly around the herring. And they are right. However, that doesn't mean you need to get bored with the food during your stay, unless you happen to be staying overnight, of course. What Finnish kitchens lack in diversity of ingredients they more than make up for in the ingenuity of their chefs. This has led to the creation of a number of dishes that are unique to Finland, including *Heirspatchoaari* (cold salted-herring soup), *Heirsparrencaaserolen* (braised herring in brine jus) and *Birdsheirspukaaren* (vodka trifle with herring and pork). Liquorice is also a popular flavouring and is added to vodka, ice cream and risotto.

Ilulissat

In the Inuit culture, the more words are used, the more they lose their power. And the less said about Greenland, the better.

Country Snapshot	
Boredom Rating	★★★★★
Likelihood of Fatal Visit	★★
Essential Packing	Good malt whisky and favourite tumbler
Most Likely Cause of Death	Frostbite

History

Historically, two big questions remain about Greenland. Firstly, what happened to the many tribes that settled there before the Thule culture became predominant? And, secondly, why did so many tribes bother to settle in the area in the first place? This second question remains a mystery to anyone who has had any experience of Greenland. As to the first, the anthropological experts who have studied the region for years are moving round to the idea that maybe the lack of sunshine, aggressive polar bears and freezing temperatures might have had something to do with what finished off the Thules and any other tribes moronic enough to have a go at making it in Greenland.

Greenland does at least benefit from a lack of the pointless battles, territorial manoeuvrings and absurd traditions that tend to dominate European history. The story of Greenland has been one of basic survival, something it's actually been doing a lot better since it left the EU and its inflation rate dropped to 1.2 percent.

Culture

Ilulissat is on the west coast of Greenland just above the Arctic Circle close to the optimistically named Disko Bay, and may well be the only city in Europe where you won't have to worry about getting enough

Don't Miss Out in Ilulissat

Head out to Uummannaq fjord for a bracing game of ice golf. Oscar Wilde famously described golf as "a good walk ruined". The people of Greenland have taken this already pointless pastime to new levels of absurdity by ensuring that the walk was actually no fun to begin with. But when it comes to pointless sports the options here are endless. With landscape too mountainous for even the briefest of pistes, cross-country is the preferred skiing form. And if you find all that moving about has a tendency to stop the blood from freezing up in your veins, why not head off ice fishing? Make sure you let your family know you may be some time though.

ice in your drink. Other than that it has little to recommend it culturally. A spoken-word tradition based on not speaking and a contemporary art world dominated by the carving of gruesome voodoo-like figures called *Tupilak* from whalebone makes it a must-go destination for only the most deranged or pretentious of cultural tourists. Even Greenpeace have given up on their attempts to curbing the whaling industry, largely because members of the organisation tend to prefer their demonstrating to be done in bits of ocean where you're able to remove your swimsuit without losing all your fingers and toes to frostbite.

But even a city where dogsleds are not just legal but pretty much essential does play host to one vital endangered species — the lesser-spotted smoker. Instead of shivering on the pavement outside their offices for the sake of a puff, workers and tourists in Illulisat can stay inside to indulge their vice, notwithstanding that inside in Greenland is generally colder than anywhere else outside on the planet.

Attractions

If after two hours of Leonardo DiCaprio's mock blarney in *Titanic* you too were rooting for the iceberg, then Ilulissat might just be for you. However, after a couple of hours watching bergs on the bay you'll probably feel like doing something non-ice related, which in Ilulissat is nigh on impossible. The Cold Museum doesn't require heat to preserve its contents, which is just as well, and from here you can organise a trip to Kafellklubben Island. This is not, as was previously thought, the end of the world – merely the most northern point. Though you may feel differently once you've been there.

Eating and Drinking

If it's big, ugly and out of the frozen sea, chances are you'll end up eating it. Make sure not to sit at the head of the table, as this is where the tastiest parts of the kill – kidneys, heart and eyes – tend to get allocated.

Istanbul

"Welcome to Hell" is a favourite greeting for many who visit Istanbul.

Boredom Rating	★ ★ ★
Likelihood of Fatal Visit	★ ★
Essential Packing	Safety pins
Most Likely Cause of Death	Over-keen masseur

History

Conquered by Alexander the Great and absorbed by the Roman Empire, Istanbul has gone through more name changes in its history than the artist formerly known as the artist formerly known as Prince. Its minaret-dotted skyline and impressive temples made Constantinople, as it was then, a must-see destination for travellers from all over Europe. Unfortunately most of them came heavily armed, and after numerous campaigns dogged by poor planning and a lack of viable sponsorship tie-ins, the forces of the Holy Crusade achieved one of their key objectives at the fourth time of asking, early in the 13th century. They celebrated the capture of arguably the greatest Christian city in the world by pillaging its treasures, destroying its churches and raping and murdering its inhabitants, regardless of their religion. Seven hundred years of recapture, rebuilding, ethnic splintering, in-fighting and all-out warring later the situation in Turkey plunged to a new low when backing the wrong side in World War I led to British occupation. The result was a country that remained politically and socially unstable but which now also had restrictive licensing laws and nowhere you could get a good cup of coffee.

Culture

After losing ground to Ankara throughout the century, Istanbul has now re-established itself as the cultural heart of Turkey. Whether this is something to be proud of or not is debatable, but Istanbul is certainly somewhere worth heading for anyone who wants to see some remarkable mosques, buy an evil eye for a family member or stay in some of the most appallingly constructed budget accommodation this side of Moscow youth hostel. But while modern developments have in many cases been slung up with little thought for design, the tone of the surrounding area or any adherence to recognised building standards, there are still things in Istanbul that have remained unchanged since elephants stopped wearing fur coats – namely an attitude to women that has given Turkey the record for the prevalence and depth of the inequality between the sexes among EU candidates. Which is just another way of saying that a husband who's not averse to giving his wife the odd slap is probably something of a catch in Turkey – it's the ones who stone, beat and murder that need to be avoided.

Attractions

Istanbul's biggest draw is a Hippodrome at which you've unfortunately very little chance of being accosted by lap dancers. The Atmeydani, as it is

A traditional Beard Seller shows his trade.

Bathing Istanbul Style

No visit to Istanbul is complete without a genuine Turkish bath, and since you'll be lucky to find a bath of any nationality in your hotel, head to Cemberlitas Hamami, one of the city's oldest bathhouses. Options available include singles and doubles and you can either do yourself or have an attendant do you. Since this is a reputable establishment you probably don't want to even think about asking for extras, unless you want to find yourself on the receiving end of some unwanted physical conditioning in the bathhouse of one of the country's notorious F-type prisons.

known, was the site of gory sporting events in pre-Galatasary days, with chariot racing frequently topping the bill. As well as providing entertainment for the Byzantium masses, they were often used to determine elections, a process modern Turks look back on with great affection as they consider the current state of political debate in the country.

Eating and Drinking

Turkish dishes have become popular the world over, bringing the kebab – cubed, skewered and griddled meat, often served in traditional bread – to your local high street. All of which saves you the misery of having to go to Turkey to experience it. Should you be unfortunate enough to end up dining in one of the city's restaurants, rest assured that the waiters will treat any females in your party with a great deal more respect than they reserve for their own countrywomen. Your tip should reflect this. Expect to pay 10 percent for good service, or 20 percent if you want the waiter to stop chatting up your wife/partner/sister/mother.

Just when Eastern Europe seemed to be losing its appetite for intrigue, conflict and internecine strife, up pops the Ukraine with a catalogue of election rigging, dirty tricks and (character) assassination not seen since... well, since Florida in 2000.

Boredom Rating	★★
Likelihood of Fatal Visit	★★
Essential Packing	Orange banner/ nothing orange whatsoever (check current situation before departure)
Most Likely Cause of Death	Gradual poisoning

History

The Ukraine's rich history is still much in evidence throughout the city of Kiev, from its Gothic cathedral spires to its Byzantine cuisine and medieval approach to customer service. A former Cossack bolthole, the country bears the unfortunate distinction of being one place on Earth where Soviet central planning actually achieved its intended aim. Stalin's engineered famine of the 1930s may have given a generation of Ukrainian women waistlines that were briefly the envy of European society, but it also left a legacy of hatred and bitterness for totalitarianism that remains to this day, not to mention a deep and abiding suspicion of low-fat spread.

Culture

The pain and sorrow of Ukrainian history are reflected throughout the culture of the people, most notably through *dumas* and *bylyny*, epic free-form narrative poems that are wailed tunelessly and can last for several days. Despite the somewhat grisly associations, Ukrainian society retains a strong sense of its socialist past, and as a result performers are chosen by an audition process based not on their vocal or musical talents but on their perceived devotion to the collective ideals of the village. This means that audiences are not given the chance to wallow in the bourgeois luxuries of tune and rhythm and can focus their attention on the raw message of the song, such as it is. Vocalists are accompanied by musicians, chosen through a similarly autonomous process, who play *banduras*, 45-string instruments, which are deliberately left un-tuned to further the collective philosophy, all notes within any musical scale being seen as having something to offer.

Attractions

St. Sophia Cathedral dominates the old town of Kiev, and in a city that has endured Mongol hordes, Soviet restructuring, Luftewaffe bombing raids and visiting English football fans, it is notable for still standing. Just. Bessarabsky market lies a few grim minutes walk from the cathedral and is the place to work on your haggling skills. Ukrainian traders can get a little bit nasty, but only if you agree to the first price they offer. Try and whittle them down a few *hryvnia* and they will show their pleasure at your engaging with one of their best-loved traditions by raising their voices, calling for help from burly, usually female, relatives and producing weapons. Flip them the bird to show your contempt for their goods, manner and family name and the fun can really start.

Eating and Drinking

The beetroot plays an almost sacred role in Ukrainian life, serving as a national symbol, source of fuel, decoration and primitive sex toy, as well as the principal ingredient of *borscht*. A soup served with cream, where available, and brake fluid everywhere else, *borscht* is as ubiquitous in Kiev as it is inedible. *Salo* – pig fat – is also incredibly popular and, like fine wine, is assigned vintages by Ukrainians, so you shouldn't feel bad about succumbing to the urge to spit it out as soon as you've tasted it.

Kosovo

With political assassinations, warring gang lords and gruesome folk music, Kosovo offers all the innocent fun of a '60s spy movie, minus the cheesy happy ending.

Boredom Rating	★
Likelihood of Fatal Visit	★★★★
Essential Packing	Marlboro cigarettes
Most Likely Cause of Death	UN Peacekeeping Force "friendly" fire

millennial celebrations in the Balkans would go with a bang whether or not the firework displays went ahead. The rest of the world took a good cop–bad cop approach to sorting things out, allowing the UN to establish a ceasefire (which was broken) and propose a settlement (which was rejected) before agreeing that maybe it would just be best to let NATO bomb the hell out of the region. The resulting conflict redefined NATO, transforming it from what was in essence a defensive alliance to an offensive fighting force. It was certainly considered offensive by the many Kosovans who wound up with al-fresco lounges as a result of NATO air strikes.

History

Just when the bloodiest century in recorded history looked to be coming to a relatively peaceful close, racial tensions that had been left to simmer nicely for a few dozen generations bubbled up and ensured

Culture

Despite – or perhaps because of – the perpetual presence of enough heavily armed peacekeeping forces to make you think the NRA are hosting a convention in town, Kosovo remains a travel

destination perfect only for those that lack motivation for continued living. Anyone with any interest in seeing their next birthday should probably think about heading somewhere a little safer, such as the top of Everest without oxygen. Still, a brief taste of Serbian folk music is likely to leave you questioning whether life is all that worth living anyway, particularly when it's played on the *gajde*, a shapeless wailing wind instrument that looks like a small person trapped in a sack. In fact, it could well be Celine Dion based on the dreadful sound it makes when it's manhandled into use.

Guca gypsy dancers haunt Kosovo's few remaining restaurants and perform energetic, semi-improvised routines that blend the Turkish, Arabic and Celtic traditions with highly innovative contemporary pick-pocketing techniques.

Attractions

Durmitor National Park is close to Montenegro's border and the region has become famous for its dramatic landscapes and outbreaks of inter-ethnic violence. The most notable feature of the park is Tara Canyon, which at 60 miles long and 3,500 feet deep remains the biggest hole in the countryside, despite the recent efforts of over-zealous US bomber pilots.

Eating and Drinking

Kosovan cuisine blends the flavours of Turkish, Hungarian and Greek cuisine into dishes of unparalleled unpalatability. Meat features heavily, from the traditional Balkan *burek*, a meat, cheese and beef-fat pie most Kosovans eat first thing, to *pihtije*, a snack made from jellied pork or duck that Kosovans tend to enjoy mid-morning after they've vomited up their breakfasts. Vegetarians should be warned that even if something is labelled as vegetarian, it might not always be, as goose fat is frequently used to thicken up soups and milkshakes. Serbian fruit is of extremely high quality but is rarely to be found in shops and restaurants as the entire national crop is used for brewing vile liqueurs.

Liverpool

The birthplace of the Beatles. The fab four showed their devotion to their home city after their international success by never returning to it again.

Danger Rating	
Boredom Rating	★★★★
Likelihood of Fatal Visit	★
Essential Packing	Reversible Liverpool/Everton football shirt
Most Likely Cause of Death	Joyrider mounting pavement

History

Historically, Liverpool has played an important role for the English – namely to be the butt of their jokes, particularly when Irishmen are present. The decline of ship building in the late 1950s has led to the emergence of new industries, and Merseysiders have proved to be a flexible workforce, quickly adapting to new roles in the car-theft, drug-dealing and benefit-fraud trades. While parts of the city – Toxteth, Walkley, the city centre, commercial district, retail centre and all the surrounding suburbs – are clearly

in economic decline, the people of Liverpool remain positive – positive that it's not their problem and there's nothing any of them can do about it anyway.

Culture

As well as the Beatles, Liverpool has a reputation for producing many of the comics and entertainers who have dominated British TV for the last 20 years – Cilla Black, Jimmy Tarbuck and Paul O'Grady all hail from the banks of the Mersey. And if you've seen any of their work you'll have a better appreciation of the loathing most Brits feel for the city and its people.

Attractions

Probably the first place for visitors to head in Liverpool is the Cavern Club – or at least the car park that was built on the site when the city council decided to demolish its potential goldmine for the sake of a pay-and-display. The best way to get over such a disappointment is to head down to the Albert Dock, a stunning new development on the Mersey waterfront just west of the town centre. Combining trendy bars, fine restaurants and the Tate Liverpool art gallery, the developers have made the centre even more attractive by fixing prices high enough to keep going there economically impossible for the vast majority of the city's inhabitants.

Eating and Drinking

Liverpudlians love the outdoors and are often to be found chatting merrily on park benches, guardedly clutching cans of industrial-strength lager – even in midwinter. Not surprisingly, eating is an informal affair and the average meal tends to be deep fried, eaten with the hands and found in a litterbin.

Liverpool Cathedral has been voted Europe's Ugliest Place of Worship a remarkable 27 times.

London

Just when Londoners thought it couldn't get any more overcrowded, they were forced to make room for a noisy and demanding group of immigrants with little respect for English culture and a rude and demanding nature. And Madonna and her entourage still show no sign of leaving.

Boredom Rating	★
Likelihood of Fatal Visit	★★
Essential Packing	Swimmer's nose clip
Most Likely Cause of Death	Food poisoning

Getting Around

London is blessed with what is not only the largest underground railway network in the world, but also the oldest – initial construction of the first station was completed in 1863, which was also the last time anyone went round with a duster down there. The "tube" – as it is affectionately known – has been bringing Londoners together for more than 140 years now and is truly a pervert's paradise – the one place where sniffing a stranger's armpits is considered not a sexual perversion but a condition of travel. For claustrophobics, London also has a large fleet of its world-famous red double-decker buses, in which visitors to the capital can sit in stationary splendour, with a perfect view of the traffic gridlocked all around them. For those who need to get somewhere, London also boasts an impressive surface rail network. Trains are generally very reliable, although delays can occur as a result of adverse weather conditions such as snow, rain, wind, cold, heat, humidity or any of the other temperate conditions you might expect to find in northern Europe at any time of year.

History

Like Betamax videos, the therapeutic use of leeches and the music of Stock, Aitken and Waterman, London probably seemed like a good idea at some point in time. Sadly, that time has now past. Like the country that surrounds it, London is a place of faded glory, the administrative centre of an evil empire long since lost, defined by outdated dogma and populated by the worst-tempered people in Europe. After the Germans, of course.

Culture

Everything in England is built around the class system and nowhere is this more in evidence than in the capital city. London is full of incredible architecture, manicured gardens and ornate palaces, and visitors to London are afforded the occasional glimpse of these through gaps in the railings and the brief occasions when the security gates are opened to allow VIP's armoured limousines out. The rest of the time, they can expect the usual round of tacky excursions, franchised interactive experiences and some of the most overpriced souvenirs on the planet. Expect to pay a 700 percent mark up on the tat you could buy anywhere else in the world for the privilege of getting a union jack on it.

Attractions

In recent years, the Royal Family of Great Britain, stung by criticisms of their lavish lifestyle, have revolutionised their approach to the public and become far more accessible. Buckingham Palace is now open for a whole eight weeks of the year, allowing the visitor to London, along with the great British public, the opportunity to get a look at the lavish artworks and antiquities they paid for in the first place. And all for the nominal charge of £12.95 (£11.00 for pensioners, £6.50 for children).

In recent years, new landmarks have sprung up around the capital. Prominent among these is the London Eye, which casts its shadow over the concrete nightmare that is the National Theatre, on the South Bank of the Thames. The Eye takes passengers on a thrilling journey over a period of around 40 minutes, reaching speeds of up to three miles per hour. As one breathless sightseer recently described it, the Eye is "like a big wheel at the fun fair, only crappier".

Eating and Drinking

Despite its claims to being a 24-hour city, outdated and unsurprisingly class-driven legislation means that unless you're lucky enough to be a member of a private club, you cannot buy a drink after 11pm (10.30pm on Sundays). While this might lead to rioting in any continental city, the bulldog Brits have kept a stiff upper lip about the situation and have made the collective decision to simply forego dinner in order to maximise their limited drinking time. So dinner is likely to be a soggy sandwich from behind the beer-soaked bar or a bag of pork scratchings – a vile pork-rind snack that was declared illegal by UN charter in 1982 and that the English are still attempting to clear a backlog of.

The fact that the nation of shopkeepers chuck their drunken patrons out on the street just as the evening is getting started means that while you may have little joy finding anywhere to eat after the pub, if you're looking for trouble, you won't have to look very far – it'll find you, particularly as London's police force seem to shut up shop at 11pm too.

This playground of the rich and formerly famous is off-limits to mere mortals.

Boredom Rating	★★★★
Likelihood of Fatal Visit	★
Essential Packing	Several credit cards
Most Likely Cause of Death	Starvation due to depleted funds

History

Like an international duelling second, Switzerland has taken on the role of looking after the jackets, and most importantly, wallets, of contesting parties wherever there is conflict. Guaranteed independence and permanent neutrality in 1815 at the Congress of Vienna after Napoleon's failed comeback tour, the Swiss were able to devote their energies to the things that really mattered in life. Why they chose cuckoo clocks and bland cheese with holes in it is one of the many mysteries of the Swiss character, but they are probably forgiven by the world's consumers for the nice chocolate they also came up with.

Switzerland was able to maintain its neutrality throughout both World Wars, and in a show of good faith was happy to accept both looted Nazi gold and the funds of European deportees alike. However, it drew the line at accepting refugees trying to escape the holocaust and to this day its immigration regulations are notoriously tight, requiring all applicants to submit full business plans, take a pledge of allegiance to the Swiss flag and yodel the National Anthem in perfect pitch backwards.

Culture

Neither German nor French, the Swiss have nonetheless taken on cultural elements of both of their larger neighbours. Combining the frosty snobbery of the French with the intolerant pomposity of the Germans has allowed the Swiss to elevate the act of ignoring people to an art form, which is just as well when you consider the general standard of Swiss attempts at all the other art forms.

Attractions

The most attractive thing about Lucerne is the lake from which it takes its name. Because it is 44 square miles in size, the local authorities have yet to find a way of charging admission to seeing it. The Dying Lion of Lucerne is nearby and was described by Mark Twain as the saddest piece of rock in the world. Visitors to Lucerne will know how it feels. The Transport Museum features the kind of interactive learning experiences that appeal to very young infants and the educationally sub-normal. Of more interest is the 360-degree cinema, which offers you the promise of a guided tour of the great Swiss outdoors without you actually having to go outdoors for it.

Eating and Drinking

Swiss cuisine is among the most inventive in the world. Using basic ingredients, Swiss chefs are able to serve up familiar foodstuffs you could buy cheaply in any market in the world, give them a needlessly complicated name and charge you extortionate amounts for it. Expect to eat cheese, bread and potatoes in the lower-priced establishments (of which there are two) and fondue, cubes of toast and rosti everywhere else.

Luxembourg City

A country so dull that it couldn't even come up with a name for its capital city.

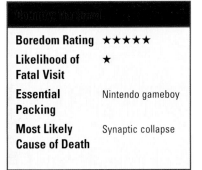

Country Information	
Boredom Rating	★★★★★
Likelihood of Fatal Visit	★
Essential Packing	Nintendo gameboy
Most Likely Cause of Death	Synaptic collapse

History

Luxembourg's history is one of a formidable castle raised and razed, of interminable sieges and bloodthirsty slaughter. All of which might be a welcome diversion from its current status as most boring place in Europe, managing to beat even its closest neighbour Belgium to the title. Granted an independence in 1830 that was ratified due to a clerical error at the signing of the Treaty of London in 1867, the citizens of the new Duchy allowed a celebratory production of *Frankenstein – The Musical* to get out of hand and as a result ended up burning down the impregnable fortress that had defined as well as defended them for centuries. Battle of the Bulge aside, this was the last thing to happen of any interest in the region, though Luxembourg did relinquish its neutrality after Nazi occupation in World War II. It has since sent several crack teams of auxiliary administrative support staff plus several highly trained chartered accountants into action on NATO's behalf as a result.

The fast minute pace of festival on the Luxquare

Culture

Visitors to Luxembourg frequently comment on how focussed their hosts seem to be on tourists. Too focussed you could say. With an entire state that's only the size of Greater London, the capital is hardly enormous, so a small-town mentality is to be expected. Look forward to the kind of intense attention you'd normally expect if you were a ten-year-old in a sweetshop looking to nick something.

And while the people of Luxembourg are probably the most linguistically learned in Europe – meaning they'll understand every word you say, regardless of what language you choose to converse in – they also speak their own dialect, *Letzebuergesch*, a tongue that's yet to appear on any syllabus anywhere else in the world. So they can chat about you knowing you'll understand not a word. The people of Luxembourg, like the aliens in *Invasion of the Bodysnatchers*, may be a little scary, but fix an emotionless half-smile on your face, keep walking and you may just trick them into thinking you're one of them.

Attractions

Probably the most remarkable sight to see in Luxembourg is the stained-glass window in the city's main train station, conveniently located 15 minutes from the city centre – which is quite an achievement in a country you can drive across in an hour. The panelling is remarkable not just for the way it looks but for the fact that it has never been damaged in the station's history, proving that even the vandals in the city err on the side of conservatism.

Eating and Drinking

Luxembourg cuisine blends the inventive sadism of a French kitchen with the double-barrelled delicacy of German cooking. Expect such treats as neck of pork with broad beans (*judd mat gaardebounen*), black blood sausage (*blutwurst*), liver dumplings (*dumpen yuucchen*) and inebriated chicken (*hahnchen im Riesling*). All served with the kind of sweet fruity wine the civilised world stopped drinking ten years ago.

Madrid

Madrid is a city where every night is party night, and it's likely to leave you feeling hungover whether you drink or not.

Light Fact Box	
Boredom Rating	★★
Likelihood of Fatal Visit	★★
Essential Packing	Blister cream
Most Likely Cause of Death	Attempting to cross the road

History

Madrid became the permanent seat of the royal court in 1561 and Felipe II then set about transforming it from a loose collection of run-down villages with no central infrastructure into a loose collection of run-down villages with no central infrastructure and a nice palace in the middle. The population quadrupled over the next few years as royal service became the number-one growth industry. More than 400 different hairdressers and beauticians were drafted into the palace in 1569, for the king alone. Despite the fact that the demand for manservants, jesters and whipping boys kept the city in near full employment, the region still lacked capital investment. This can be attributed largely to the series of disastrous military campaigns embarked upon by successive Spanish rulers. To this day Spain has a reputation for being unlucky in battle and it remains the only country in the world ever to have lost its own civil war.

Culture

Madrid is Europe's highest city and the thinness of the air may go some way to explaining the somewhat unpredictable behaviour of its inhabitants. Added to this, the Spanish tradition of *siesta* (disappearing for a kip in the middle of the afternoon) can make it difficult for visitors to adapt to the Madrid lifestyle, which combines a love of late-night carousing with a relaxed attitude to getting to work on time and to staying awake once you're there. Restaurants won't accept a booking before a time by which most people would already be tucked up in bed, and the streets only start to empty of late-night revellers as the school buses start their morning rounds. This is fine for anyone who considers nightlife the right life, but can be a problem should you require competency from anyone you engage professionally. Taxi drivers stray all over the roads and waiters are likely to forget your order and then spill it down you when it does arrive.

Attractions

The Prado contains more than 7,000 works of art and is constantly introducing new works by new artists – so there should be something of interest on show there soon. Sports fans who enjoy witnessing the crazed taunting of a vicious mob are well catered for by Plaza de Toros de Las Ventas, the world's largest bullfighting ring, or can watch any football match at the Bernabeu featuring non-Caucasian players.

Eating and Drinking

Once your body clock has adjusted to Madrid Time it's worth experiencing a night in one of Madrid's many restaurants. Booking is not essential, but popular ones become crowded and smoky very quickly, particularly during Spain's many public holidays, which include *La Inmaculada Concepción* (Feast of the Immaculate Conception) on December 8th, *La Asunción* (Feast of the Assumption) on August 15th and *Fiesta del Subsequentos* (Festival of the Day After Yesterday), which is celebrated weekly.

Magaluf

British families have been flocking to the Costa Del Sol in their thousands since the 1970s. None with any discernible taste ever return.

Country Spain	
Boredom Rating	★★★
Likelihood of Fatal Visit	★★★
Essential Packing	Face mask (or any means of concealing identity)
Most Likely Cause of Death	Beating from nightclub bouncer

History

It's difficult to know who to blame for Magaluf, which is probably the most depressing and disgusting of all the resorts on Spain's notorious Costa Del Sol. The cheap Spanish package holidays that became available in the 1970s were such a success it was only natural for tour operators to respond to the sudden demand for a fortnight in what must have seemed like paradise to many northern Europeans. Sadly, the local market also encouraged the worst instincts of their new customers, who were only too happy to soak up the climate but had little truck with local customs, culture or food. Like Las Vegas – albeit on a smaller, grubbier, more European scale – the Costa del Sol's primary function is to serve as a vital reminder to us all of just where the free market system will go if you let it. Oh, and also to provide somewhere for British gangsters to retire to.

Sadly the donkey figurines tucked away at the back of the gift shop were tiny.

Culture

Walking through Magaluf is like entering a parallel dimension – one where the earth has been tilted on its axis to put the UK a mere 15 degrees or so above the equator. In this more temperate climate, Brits are able to take a leaf out of their US cousins' book and never leave home, even to go on holiday. For Magaluf is a town almost entirely devoid of Spanish culture. Where it does exist – the faint strains of frantic guitar music coming from the laundry block of your hotel, the flamenco dancer figurines stashed away at the back of the gift shop behind the football shirts and novelty donkeys – it's unobtrusive and apologetic about being there in the first place. What is to the fore are those very elements of English culture most people have paid hard-earned pounds to get away from in the first place – dark smoky pubs, karaoke machines and loud children made hyperactive by a constant diet of Micro Chips and Sunny Delight.

Attractions

Magaluf boasts several of the largest nightclubs in the region, at least one of which is bound to be within earshot of your hotel. Fusion offers free booze once you've paid your admission, and subsequently offers the least attentive bar staff serving the most watered-down beer in Europe, while Massive boasts a winning combination of disinterested cage dancers and intolerant bouncers in case masochism should happen to be your bag.

Eating and Drinking

A night in a Tapas bar is, of course, one great way to eat, drink and be sociable with friends that won't be available should you choose Magaluf as your holiday destination. However, if a traditional English meal three times a day is your idea of heaven, Magaluf is certainly the place for you. Just remember to pack your donor card. The Benny Hill Bar is a great place for a quiet pint or 12 before getting into a fight, eating a kebab and falling asleep in the gutter.

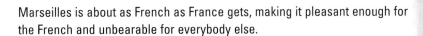

Marseilles

Marseilles is about as French as France gets, making it pleasant enough for the French and unbearable for everybody else.

Boredom Rating ★★	
Likelihood of Fatal Visit	★★★
Essential Packing	French Foreign Legion application form
Most Likely Cause of Death	Dockside knife fight

History

Marseilles is, has been for 26 centuries and no doubt ever shall be a stinking port on the south coast of France that attracts all the very worst elements of society. The city is defined by the docks, which also provide most of the employment opportunities and all of the seedy local colour. Heavy moustaches, tattoos and scars are *de rigueur*, and male travellers may also want to think about amputating a finger, ear or leg in order to really be accepted by the local population.

Marseilles has fought its image as a place to be avoided at all costs ever since it became the plague's point of entry to mainland Europe in 1720. The battle is all but lost. For Hollywood, and therefore the rest of the dumb movie-going world, Marseilles is a crime-infested sleaze-pit with corrupt officials and poor sanitation. Even French viewers who dismissed *The French Connection* movies as being *trop fantastique* (unbelievable) admitted that their main reason for doing so was the fact that the police in the film were engaged in investigative work rather than just sitting outside cafés smoking Gauloises and making lurid approaches to female passers-by.

Culture

Marseilles is not France's capital, but don't try mentioning that to anyone living there – Provençe is to France what the Midwest is to the US. And the Provençe city that gave the country its national anthem has a tendency to see itself in even more self-inflated terms. It's certainly the case that many of the classic characteristics of Gallic behaviour are in abundance in the attitude of the townsfolk. So the same arrogance that allows French premiers to linger in office way past their sell-by date can be seen in the way shopkeepers will chat for hours with their regular customers while the baguette you're trying to buy gets sweaty in your palm. The same respect for the environment shown by the French military during their World War III rehearsal on the Polynesian island of Mururoa is evident in the way your minicab driver casually pulls up and takes a piss by the roadside as you sit inside watching the meter tot up. You should learn to put up with such charming eccentricities and by no means challenge them, as this will be seen as extremely rude.

Attractions

To say that Marseilles has a beach is stretching the limits of the word, but it does have a place where you can walk by the sea that isn't a pavement. You can get there by heading to the Calanques – a series of steep narrow inlets where creeks join the sea. A treacherous stroll down these rewards the intrepid walker with an equally uninviting beach made up of jagged pebbles and a tide that can turn on you like a rabid St. Bernard.

Festivals and Provence

July 14th is a great day to be in Marseilles. Unlike the rest of France, the children of Marseilles celebrate Bastille Day by making it the one day of the calendar year when they don't throw firecrackers at people on the street. Needless to say, normal service resumes on the 15th.

Anyone not liking fish in Marseilles will quickly develop a taste for it – or starve.

Eating and Drinking

Marseilles cuisine is dominated by the flavours of the sea and the French penchant for garlic, and you can guarantee that whatever you order will come with the pungent aroma of spicy fish. This makes for fantastic *bouillabaisse* but not so fantastic *crème brûlée* and absolutely undrinkable coffee.

The city of Moscow has made it through war, revolution and the collapse of communism. Whether or not it can survive the onslaught of its own citizens finally off the leash after centuries of repression remains to be seen.

Country Russian Federation

Boredom Rating	★★
Likelihood of Fatal Visit	★★★★
Essential Packing	Wedding ring – regardless of whether you're married or single
Most Likely Cause of Death	Mafiosi hit

History

Moscow has been at the centre of Russian life for 1,000 years. It's survived sacking by the Tatar hordes, invasion by Napoleon's army and not really being liked very much by Peter the Great, who did all he could to relocate the Russian court to St. Petersburg.

But while modestly self-titled Russian leaders have come and gone, Moscow has remained the beating heart of the nation, with the Kremlin serving as the stronghold of Russian political power. It was from here that, in the 20th century alone, Lenin made the dictatorship of the proletariat; Stalin orchestrated his bloody purges; Khrushchev took the planet to the brink of nuclear conflict; Gorbachev ushered in the new dawn of *perestroika*; and Yeltsin got so plastered he decided to abandon the project and sign away power altogether.

Culture

The clues to understanding Russian culture are to be seen wherever you go in Moscow. The Tsar Bell and Tsar Cannon are both to be found in Cathedral Square. Both are large-scale constructions that are impressive from a distance, but on closer inspection they're aged and broken. And since the Tsar Bell was

Method of Wackiness

The cultural impact of the Moscow Arts Theatre on western dramatic art cannot be underestimated. It was founded in 1898 by Konstantin Stanislavsky and Vladimir Nemirovich-Danchenko, whose goal was to establish a theatre of new art forms. Its fresh approach to performance allowed the theatre to abandon its stuffy bourgeois preoccupations and adopt a realism in writing and performance that we take for granted today, but was revolutionary in its time. Actors were encouraged to fully explore their characters and to imbue their portrayals with a focus on reality, rather than use them to gratuitously showcase their own talents as performers. The remarkable body of work left for us by Marlon Brando, whose insightful nuances and on-screen intensity electrified audiences, is one legacy of the innovation of the Moscow Arts approach. So, too, are the inaudible mumblings and self-absorbed preening of Stephen Dorff, which continue to nauseate audiences to this day, illustrating that there are always down sides to even the best ideas.

never rung and the Tsar Cannon was never fired, like all too many things in Russia's socialist past, neither has ever served any practical purpose.

But while Soviet experiments in political science may have now floundered, the Russian people have embraced the freedom that has come with whatever mechanism it is exactly that's replaced their once centrally planned economy. One place where this change is evident is Gorky Park. Situated on the right

Novodevichy Convent is the place to find the final resting places of many of history's most famous Russians: Chekov, Eisenstein, Gogol, Profokiev, Stanislavsky and Shostakovich are all buried here, an honour bestowed only on Russia's truly great or hugely wealthy. Of course, getting a marked grave at all is considered a major status symbol in the country that pioneered the technique of losing its dissidents in the remoter parts of its countryside, which is easily done when those regions of the world exist in almost perpetual darkness and get a metre of snow a day.

bank of the Moskva River just beyond Crimea Bridge, it was once a desolate and deserted place that most Muscovites had neither the time nor the inclination to take advantage of. But soaring unemployment rates have given people the chance to appreciate their freedom, and a morning stroll through the untended gardens is now a now a heart-warming experience. By 10am even remote corners of the park are dotted with Russians clutching bottles of 100-percent-proof parsnip vodka and happily singing to themselves.

Attractions

Moscow also boasts a number of amusement parks where the same Eastern European engineering skills that made sure the Russian Space Shuttle *Buran* never made it off the ground meets all the decadent fun of a bargain-basement Busch Gardens. This has resulted in some of the world's most unintentionally scary thrill rides yet to be closed down by health and safety authorities.

Eating and Drinking

Going out for dinner in Moscow used to be a dismal affair – cavernous dining rooms, lousy food and a walk home along city streets that were deserted by 9pm. Most of that has now changed. The food may still be lousy, but the rise of the Russian Mafiosi means that wherever you chose to eat in the evening is likely to be a front for something else and so you're in for an interesting evening. On a good night you'll think you've been whisked back to Chicago of the '30s. Bodyguards squaring up to each other, catfights between molls and armed kidnappings are all made more interesting by the fact that by nightfall even the most clean-living Muscovite will have consumed a half bottle of vodka. Smokers will be delighted to hear that cigarettes and cigars are encouraged in Moscow's restaurants, mainly since they help cover the smell of all the cordite.

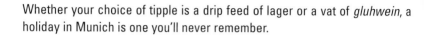

Munich

Whether your choice of tipple is a drip feed of lager or a vat of *gluhwein*, a holiday in Munich is one you'll never remember.

Country Guide	
Boredom Rating	★★
Likelihood of Fatal Visit	★
Essential Packing	Bottle opener
Most Likely Cause of Death	Lager-inspired stupidity

Munich – Party Town!

Plans are underway for building on the city's reputation for vibrant nightlife. The Department of Tourism is particularly keen to ape the success of the Rhine's famous festivals, such as the Rhine in Flames, where water, *son et lumiere* and fireworks are used to create a dazzling spectacle. However, their plans for a Beer House in Flames event to run alongside *Oktoberfest* were recently rejected on the grounds of health and safety.

History

When it comes to players on the world stage, no nation comes close to touching the impact that Germany has had on the world. In the last century alone it was home to the forces directly responsible for the two largest international armed conflicts, a record that the US has coveted ever since and looks determined to beat in the very near future. But post-war, it has turned its undisputed talents for engineering and organisation to business with a great deal of success in both the private and public sector. The BMW marque has become a symbol of German efficiency that is known and loathed the world over. And Germans enjoy the benefits of one of the most advanced transport networks in the developed world. German *autobahns* are the envy of scary drivers everywhere and while there are only a few sections of highway with a restrictive speed

limit, it reports very few fatalities. This is due to the high level of safety features in the standard German family saloon. While this will be of little use to you in your cheap Italian budget rental car, you can at least draw some comfort from knowing that the guy in the Porsche Boxster who was doing 155mph when he hit you will probably escape with his life if not his full set of limbs. Much to the disappointment of bloodthirsty German drivers, cyclists are strictly forbidden from the *autobahn*.

Culture

What passes for culture in Germany would pass for insanity anywhere else in the world – grown men strolling the streets of the *aldstadt* (old town) in leather shorts and dinky green hats; a guttural language that sounds even worse to the ear than it looks on the page; and Beethoven, of course. Central to this is a surprisingly high level of tolerance. The first European member of the International Gay and Lesbian Travel Association, Munich lays claim to being one of the most gay-and-lesbian friendly cities on Earth. And *Oktoberfest* – the world's largest beer festival – has united Germany despite its troubled past, giving lager-louts of every nation the chance to come together annually to show that, despite their apparent national differences, under the skin they're all a bunch of sub-literate morons.

Attractions

The reputation Germany has for lacking a sense of humour would seem misplaced based on the naming of at least one Munich attraction. The English Garden is Europe's largest city park, and as well as housing several *pilsner* bars and a totally out-of-place Chinese Tower, it is also a haven for Munich's growing community of naturalists. Any repressed Brit that enters the park for an innocent stroll is likely to leave very quickly in a flurry of coughs and splutters at the sight of so many sunbathers singeing their naked flesh like *wurst* under a grill.

Eating and Drinking

The German diet has traditionally revolved around sausage meat and tankards of strong beer, but many Germans are now seeking to reduce their calorific intake and replacing sausages with offal dumplings and drinking only lite beer at breakfast.

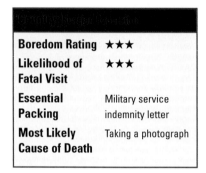

Murmansk

You've got to work hard to be considered the most miserable part of Russia, which makes Murmansk the most Stakhanovite city in Russia.

Boredom Rating	★★★
Likelihood of Fatal Visit	★★★
Essential Packing	Military service indemnity letter
Most Likely Cause of Death	Taking a photograph

History

Founded in 1916, Murmansk is the largest Russian seaport on the Arctic Ocean. Subsequently, it has historically been a place associated with misery as Russian *babushkas* said goodbye to their sailor sons, young lolitas said goodbye to their sweethearts and submariners said goodbye to the prospect of encountering daylight for a couple of months. Not that Murmansk is famous for its sunlight.

Known as Romanov-on-Murman before the Revolution in 1917, it is said to take its name from the Russian form of the name Norman. And therein lies all you really need to know about Murmansk, a strange and potentially dangerous place kept in secluded misery by the overbearing effects of a long-dead mother country it can't bring itself to bury.

Culture

When you're surrounded on three sides by icy tundra, you're not likely to have residents who moved in because they like the scenery. The main base of the country's fishing industry, Murmansk also still plays host to a number of military establishments, many of which prefer to keep themselves to themselves. This brings a whole world of potential inconvenience for anyone disturbed enough to want to take photos as souvenirs of their trip. The city may seem as empty, but with nearly seven and a half people per square kilometre it's actually a tighter squeeze than most of Russia. In any case, you'll soon be feeling the squeeze if you should happen to snap a shot of one of the many unmarked security establishments that litter the city. Bear in mind that most Murmans – security guards, military officials and interrogators alike – don't speak English. Or French, German, Finnish, Swedish, or even any form of Russian that any Russians would admit to understanding.

Attractions

The Kola Nuclear Power Plant is the pride of Murmansk, producing not only all of the region's electricity but also nearly two percent of the electricity for the country as a whole, as well as selling its product to nearby Karelia and Finland. And why not round off your tour of the facility with a can of the factory's very own soft drink. Made with local spring water and real artificial flavourings, Kola Cola is naturally carbonated and tends to be served piping hot for reasons no one is too clear about.

Eating and Drinking

Kalitki – or "pockets" – are local specialities that are served with your choice of vegetables – providing your choice is potatoes. It's hard to see why the locals like these things, which have the texture and flavour of discarded and thumb-worn pieces of material, but their popularity may at least explain why no one in Murmansk ever seems to have any money.

The Gateway to Siberia is best seen through the frosty window of a speeding train bearing you to the (relative) delights of Moscow – or anywhere else.

Boredom Rating	★★★
Likelihood of Fatal Visit	★★★
Essential Packing	Empty salt cellar
Most Likely Cause of Death	Paddling in the Irytush

History

Discoveries made in Siberia during the 1990s indicate that the region may have been inhabited for as long as 300,000 years. What's certain is that no one stuck around for long. As a starting point for campaigns by Mongols, Manchus and Huns, it was not surprisingly taken with little resistance and discarded with little thought. However, the reason for Siberia being such a dreadful place in which to try and eke out an existence became clear when some bright sparkski hit upon the idea of using it as a penal colony. Finding somewhere even less hospitable to human life than the rest of Russia was quite a discovery and the authorities began shipping dissidents and prisoners out there in earnest. Little changed in the snowy wasteland until the Revolution, when Czarist counterrevolutionary White Army forces took control. They discovered that holding Siberia in real life was no more useful than holding it in a game of Risk and by 1920 had all deserted, been executed or sentenced to hard labour in their former bolt-hole.

Culture

Omsk owes its greatest cultural heritage to the various inmates who have done hard time there. Dostoevsky spent four years here, and was flogged to within an inch of his life for commenting on a lump of dirt in his soup – his remarks did admittedly lead to a riot by unhappy inmates who wanted dirt in theirs too.

Attractions

Siberia was at the centre of Stalin's post-war five- and seven-year plans for industry and agriculture. And the Soviets certainly did their best to ruin a part of the world that already looked as bad as things can get. The second largest city in Siberia, Omsk was also the site of the second-worst crash in the history of state civil airline Aeroflot, in 1994. As a mark of respect, city authorities have not put up signposts to the crash site. Or to anywhere else in the city, either.

Eating and Drinking

The people of Siberia take their vodka drinking very seriously. While the rawest of spirits will go down well in this harsh climate, travellers may want to develop a system for disposing of their booze without drinking it, as refusing a drink with your host can cause offence, but vomiting on him is usually grounds for duelling with ice picks.

The women of Omsk have taken to online dating with a vengeance. In a recent online survey, users of the www.siberianbrides.com site voted the women of Omsk the most likely to post a fake picture and then do a runner as soon as they'd got their hands on cash/bonds/deeds to the house.

Oslo

Oslo is such a compact little city that if you blink you'll be in danger of missing it. In fact, if you keep your eyes firmly shut you might be lucky enough to miss Norway altogether.

Boredom Rating	★★★
Likelihood of Fatal Visit	★
Essential Packing	Eye mask/number of local Samaritans' help line
Most Likely Cause of Death	Sleep deprivation (summer) / suicide (winter)

History

The Norwegians have been trying to get Oslo right for centuries. The oldest of all the Scandinavian capital cities, today's Oslo might be better named Oslo (version 3.1). Whether or not they're getting close to a finished product yet is a matter of opinion, but the current version does at least benefit from not being ridden with bubonic plague (version 1.0) or being a fire hazard (version 2.0). Or worst of all being blessed, as it was in 1925, with the title of a King with a stupid girl's name (version 3.0, or Christiana as it is sometimes referred to). Norway played its neutral card at the start of World War II, for all the good it did them, but it benefited post-war from the discovery of oilfields in the North Sea. On its day, it might be considered one of the most pleasant cities on the planet. However, the fact that that day may be one where the sun chooses either never to rise or, even worse, never to set, could make it one of either death-like blackness or unending harshness.

Culture

Oslo boasts clean air, a climate that's friendly by Scandinavian standards, some nice enough old buildings, a generally high standard of living and some kind of artistic tradition. Unfortunately, this

Getting the Munchies

Fortunately for Norway, one man was able to look past the pleasant exterior and overwhelming niceness of the region and see the misery that lurked beneath the surface. Edvard Munch grew up in Oslo and reflected his life experience in some of the bleakest paintings you're ever likely to be visually assaulted by. The Munch Museum is at Toyengata 53 and contains such memorably depressing works as "The Sick Child", "Red Virginia Creeper", and no less than 50 versions of his most famous work, "The Scream". Bleak it may be, but you'll be comforted by the fact that it's not just you that finds life in Oslo so oppressive you want to cry out about it.

combination of qualities makes the Norwegians the most unbearably smug people that you'll meet anywhere in Scandinavia. Don't be taken in by the fact that they seem to be interested enough in your hometown to ask you questions about it – being quizzed on whether you have such beautiful fjords where you live is not a genuine question whether you're from Birmingham or Biloxi. It's just a way of reminding you how attractive their surroundings are compared to yours.

Attractions

A short tram ride from the centre of Oslo you'll find a concept in public parks unique to Norway. Frognerparken is a lush and well-kept park that houses an outdoor collection of nearly 200 sculptures by renowned artist Gustav Vigeland and is the most popular attraction in the country. Vigeland's works capture the everyday and make them sublime: enraptured lovers sharing an innocent picnic lunch;

elderly figures reminiscing on that which has passed them by; hungry tramps despairing as to where their next drink might be coming from – all are captured here in stunning detail. (Due to the park's status as an important tourist draw, picnicking, petting, begging and loitering are not permitted at any time.)

Eating and Drinking

Oslo restaurants have a reputation for being dull and expensive that is well earned. However, the presence of reindeer steaks on most menus might make Oslo the perfect place to break the news to your kids that Santa isn't real. "Would you like some mustard on Rudolph, dear?"

You know that something is seriously wrong with a city when the only place you can get strong beer is from a state off-licence. The Vinmonopolet is probably the best place to pick up some 40-percent-proof aquavit as well, as the bill for a small glass of it in your hotel is likely to affect your heart rate more immediately than the drink itself will.

Paphos

The Berlin Wall has crumbled, Republicans and Unionists in Northern Ireland continue to look for ways to put past troubles behind them. But there are still some parts of the world where the only way to resolve the differences between two sets of people is to build a bloody great wall between them.

Boredom Rating	★★★★
Likelihood of Fatal Visit	★
Essential Packing	Protective eyewear (fluorescent blue rinses are prevalent)
Most Likely Cause of Death	Confusing Turkish and Greek culture

Reason for Danger

It's illegal for tourists to travel back and forth across the Green Line, so at least you'll have an excuse for not exploring both sides of the island.

History

The island of Cyprus has changed hands like an unwanted Christmas gift for most of its colourful history. Romans and Egyptians, Alexander the Great and Richard the Lionheart, German Sun-Lounger Hoarders and Obnoxious British Stag Parties have all held sway there in their time, though never for very long. The Knights Templar bought the isle in 1191, and hung onto it for the three centuries it took them to establish that – contrary to the seller's description – it wasn't the resting place of the Holy Grail.

The concept of self-determination finally occurred to the Cypriot people in the early 20th century, by which time it had come under British control. The British authorities recognised the potential for conflict between the majority Greek Cypriot population, who wanted a union with Greece, and the Turkish Cypriot minority, who didn't, and so drafted a new constitution that neither side was too crazy about and then got the hell out of Cyprus. The arrival of a UN Peacekeeping Force served as the traditional portent of doom for the notable lack of peace that followed, culminating in a whole bunch of mayhem in 1974 that the CIA picked up the tab for.

Culture

The upshot of all this is an island divided not so much by hate as by annoyance. The northern third of the island remains under Turkish Cypriot control in an independent state recognised by Turkey and no one else; the southern chunk is occupied by Greek Cypriots and hapless elderly tourists looking to save money on their package deal. The Green Line, an imposing border manned by armed guards, runs through Lefkosia or Nicosia, depending on what side of the wall you're on, and serves as the landing that's keeping the two feuding kids in their respective rooms. Only the prospect of getting them both to come down for dinner on the EU gravy train offers any chance of the two sides getting together to say sorry. All of which is of great concern to the EU, which is keen to welcome Cyprus to the international negotiating table as President Tassos Papadopoulos was voted premier whose name was most fun to say.

Attractions

Paphos markets itself as the most unspoilt resort on the island, which shows just how much spoiling has gone on since the tour operators earmarked it for homogenisation. Below-par golf courses nestle behind mid-rise hotel developments that look as if they've been flown over from a Polish housing estate and given a coat of white paint. Bad tiling and urgent repair jobs pass for mosaics and ruins and most restaurants offer artery-blocking full English breakfasts all day.

The Baths of Aphrodite are worthy of particular mention. Recently named the worst signposted attraction in the Mediterranean, they lie a mere hour and a half's white-knuckle drive up the coast from Paphos. Park your rental car, leave it unlocked and ensure valuables are clearly on show so that you won't need to pay for broken windows after the inevitable break-in, and set off up the Akamas Peninsula for a sight as unimpressive as any you're likely to come across. The leaking faucet suspended above a stagnant pond is allegedly where Aphrodite, the Greek goddess of love, bathed before her marriage to Adonis, the most handsome man ever to have lived. While running water is not always to be relied upon on the island, you can't help but think she could have found a grotto with a little less grot and slightly clearer *eau* without too much trouble.

Eating and Drinking

The fact that Paphos is a package tour destination catering to the older end of the market can make things a little difficult for the casual visitor. While you can rejoice that your sentence is not for a fixed period and you can leave whenever you want, finding somewhere to eat can prove hard, particularly in the off-season (September–May). Some of the hotels will let non-residents eat in their restaurant if you ask courteously and pay a hefty premium and on balance this is probably a better option than starving to death. Most mid-priced Paphos hotels specialise in all-you-can-eat buffets, knowing that a couple of mouthfuls of any dish is all you'll want to eat. Look out for the many *Mezedes* (appetisers), which are colourful and varied in appearance and bland and indistinguishable from each other in flavour.

Like the worst type of cute girl on a date, Paris knows what she has to offer and makes you feel stupid, ugly and unworthy and then gets you to pay through the nose for the privilege of spending time with her.

Boredom Rating	★
Likelihood of Fatal Visit	★★
Essential Packing	Most humble face
Most Likely Cause of Death	Misdirected champagne cork

History

Paris is a city steeped in the past. From the majestic beauty of Notre Dame cathedral to the brittle, curling edges of the croissant you're about to get ripped off for, history lurks in the most unexpected places.

Whether it's a romantic stroll along the banks of the Seine, a nail-biting trip to the top of the Eiffel Tower or an afternoon's indulgence in the sensory all-you-can-eat buffet of the Louvre, there's no end to the disappointments on offer to anyone visiting the city of (self) love. Because for all its attractions, Paris is full to the brim with two things that should push the city to the top of anyone's list of places to avoid: other tourists and Parisians.

Culture

France has given so much to the world – the sparkling wine we all now associate with celebration, a proper appreciation of the artistry of Jerry Lewis and a language where even "you fancy kipping here tonight?" sounds like poetry – that the world doesn't know where to start thanking it. So it simply hasn't bothered. This has made the already-quite-into-themselves French by far the most irritable people in Europe, if not the world.

Parisians are fiercely patriotic and do not take kindly to tourists assuming that they will understand English. Expect to see a blank look, some aggressive shrugging, a good deal of philosophical harrumphing and then a tirade directed at you in the native tongue for the benefit of anyone listening. The search continues for anything that a Parisian will take kindly to, but in the meantime you can do your bit to soothe French pride by learning a few words of the language. A few short phrases will do, and don't worry about learning them too precisely since any Parisian will still claim to have no idea what you are talking about. However, the blank look, shrugging and tirade will all be delivered with a wry smile, and if your pronunciation is truly terrible you may even manage to get a few laughs and thereby win your audience over with your sheer ineptitude.

Attractions

Forget all about attempting to do the big tourist draws unless you're in training for a most-people-in-a-phone-box world-record attempt. The Louvre is particularly unbearable thanks to the five percent of Americans that actually leave their own country occasionally all deciding to head for Paris clutching dog-eared copies of *The Da Vinci Code*.

The Arc de Triomphe, however, is in plenty of space and is worth a look, though building the world's largest traffic roundabout in a city where drivers clearly have no understanding of the concept would seem to be another continental example of style triumphing over practicality. Commissioned in 1806 to commemorate Napoleon's imperial victories, the slightly shorter than average French working week meant that it took 30 years to finish. This meant that Old Boney was exactly that by the time it was complete, having been exiled, returned to power, banished again and then died in the meantime.

Eating and Drinking

One of the legacies of the Reign of Terror that saw the bulk of France's ruling class dragged off for impromptu head- and neck-ectomies is a cuisine based around sadism. The French like to know that

their dinner has suffered the cruellest of journeys to make it to their dinner plate – freshly boiled (alive) lobster, veal that's just had a tearful farewell from its mother, *foie gras* from overstuffed geese. But the presence of *l'escargot* on the French dinner table would seem to suggest that the animals are finally getting their own back.

A language within a language: French shrugs within French

While French is an easy enough language to learn, mastering each of the 38 different Gallic shrugs, which are used for nuance and emphasis, remains an art that the French alone comprehend.

Reykjavik

When the days are as dull as they are in Reykjavik, it's really no wonder they make the nights so long.

Country Factors	
Boredom Rating	★★★
Likelihood of Fatal Visit	★★
Essential Packing	Normal music
Most Likely Cause of Death	Unprovoked Bjork attack

Adults Only!

Travellers who are free of the burden of holidaying with children – and who have a taste for the bizarre – will no doubt be drawn to visit Iceland's very own phallological museum, the Reoasafn, a museum that was both conceived by, and built to house, a collection of penises.

History

Iceland resisted human habitation for many years – indeed, with a summer temperature that can soar up to the mid-40s (Fahrenheit) it's easy to wonder why it became populated at all. Irish monks, unsociable Vikings and disorientated Swedes all briefly made their homes on the island, but the combination of harsh winters, unpredictable volcanic geysers and plague epidemics ensured that the country spent many centuries about as densely populated as a Moscow branch of Alcoholics Anonymous.

Things improved in the 18th century with the granting of a market town charter by the Danish government, a move that was cemented by the removal of international trade barriers in the mid-19th century. However, both of these measures were largely symbolic, as Iceland had nothing to trade until the early 20th century when the development of flavoured fruit syrups made them the number-one exporter of slushy ice drinks on the planet.

Culture

Despite boasting all the trappings of a modern city, Reykjavik still retains the atmosphere of a small village. This would normally be a good thing. However, in the case of Reykjavik, the village in question is Salem's Lot. A town cloaked in almost perpetual darkness, it's understandably dispirited residents wander the streets during its brief hours of daylight like so many weary undead. While this may make the town a little on the dull side, it does at least provide an explanation for the somewhat erratic behaviour of Iceland's most famous export, former lead singer of the Sugarcubes and renowned solo artist Bjork. For years her unique vocal performances and idiosyncratic philosophy were put down to mere eccentricity on her part. However, seen in the context of her hometown, a place where an average December day can consist of getting out of bed, having a shower and then realising it's time to go back to bed, it's clear that poor Bjork has actually been suffering the effects of acute sleep deprivation for many years. This is particularly in evidence on the later part of her difficult second album, where she is clearly enduring a narcoleptic fit that is, somewhat ironically, likely to so terrify any unfortunate listener that they, too, will be unable to sleep for a week.

Attractions

If you're looking for some laughs, head for Fjolskyldugarourinn and Husdyragarourinn. Just hearing your attempts at pronouncing the name of this fun park is likely to have any of the residents you ask for directions in stitches. Should you be lucky enough to get there, you'll find a zoo with no lions, tigers, elephants or any other creature capable of surviving in anything but Arctic conditions.

With landscapes like this, it's no wonder Bjork sounds so pained.

Eating and Drinking

There's a distinctly nautical feel to much of the cuisine on offer in Reykjavik and one taste of many of the dishes on offer will be sufficient to give you an idea of what the sailors who discovered Iceland fed on – probably just before the first instances of cannibalism broke out. Salted mutton, salted cabbage and salted squirming slug are all on the menu and can (hopefully) be washed down with a flagon of *brennivin* (burnt wine). First one to finish gets a glass of Black Death schnapps. Last to finish gets a whole bottle.

Riga combines a number of bland buildings with areas of unremarkable countryside, a featureless coastline and a few poorly maintained roads to devastatingly dull effect.

Country facts	
Boredom Rating	★★★★★
Likelihood of Fatal Visit	★★
Essential Packing	Bumper book of word-search puzzles
Most Likely Cause of Death	Coma

History

For such a bunch of international non-entities, the Latvians have certainly had a fight or two in their day. Former trading and sparring partners of the Romans, Vikings and Russians, the heathens of the region ran rampant until the 13th century. A papal crusade was launched in 1290 with the aim of converting the barbarous tribes to the charity, compassion and love inherent in Christian belief. This was done by the distinctly un-Christ like Knights of the Sword, whose distinctive garb of a blood red cross on white was later adopted by the English Football Association when designing the national strip.

Latvians mark their brief summer with numerous festivals to celebrate their all-too-short respite from icy winds and driving rain. Midsummer celebrations, which begin on June 23rd, are marked with the hanging of wreaths of flowers and herbs that are said to keep away evil spirits. They also help to mask the smell of traditional Latvian cooking.

After enjoying a few brief years of independence between the two World Wars, Latvia entered the Soviet sphere of influence and gained all the benefits that came with being subject to the usual Stalinist calling cards of purging, deportation and mass executions. World War II brought Nazi conquest, Red Army re-conquest and turnip rationing, the latter denying Latvians both the mainstay of their diet and, in its funnier shaped forms, one of their primary sources of entertainment.

Having finally achieved genuine independence from one militarily aggressive, culturally repressive, economically draining super state at the end of the 20th century, Latvia wasted no time in applying for NATO and EU membership, both of which were, not surprisingly, approved in 2004.

Culture

For many cultural connoisseurs, Latvia is made up of a series of dynamic tensions that represent the clash of cultures and ideologies that have coloured its history. For most of us, though, it's just plain confused. Like many European capitals, Riga is formed of an old town and a new town – on paper at least. Spotting the differences between the two may present something of a challenge given that Riga Cathedral is constructed out of the kind of red brick you're likely to see in a small local library or STD clinic back home. Generally speaking, you should be able to tell whether you're in the old town or the new by whether the crumbling buildings around you are made of brick and stone (old) or concrete and papier mâché (new).

Latvian music and literature are largely unknown outside the country's borders and rarely enjoyed within them. *Dainas* are folk verses that take the concept of the short Japanese poem known as the *haiku* and focus on the brevity at the expense of the poetry – perfect for anyone who prefers their tedium to be in bite-size doses.

Attractions

Latvia has been blessed with a surplus of beautifully preserved and romantically named castles and palaces. Sadly, none of them are in Riga. Leave the centre of town and your choices are between a crummy half-empty business zone and a dilapidated and bleak residential zone.

House of the Blackheads is on Melngalvju Nams and, despite its name, is not devoted to a history of teenage skin complaints through the ages, though it could hardly be less interesting if it were. Canoeing is popular with first-time visitors, but once they've capsized and sampled icy Latvian water it tends to be an activity dropped from the itinerary.

Eating and Drinking

Restaurants range from the grim austerity of old-style eastern-bloc cafeterias to trendy "new-wave" Latvian bistros with experimental menus. Both serve Riga Black Balsam, a local drink which doubles as an excellent hair dye and dandruff-control shampoo.

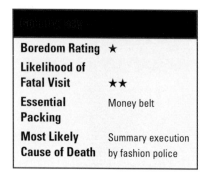

Italy's Eternal City once dominated the world culturally, but now it's best known for its pickpockets, stray cats and overpriced espresso.

Boredom Rating	★
Likelihood of Fatal Visit	★★
Essential Packing	Money belt
Most Likely Cause of Death	Summary execution by fashion police

History

For centuries, Rome has housed the headquarters of a secretive society, which through the use of violence, extortion and blackmail has extended a terrifying grip over the entire planet. However, since Vatican City is technically a nation state in its own right and didn't make it into the top 101, we'll have to leave it for the next edition.

Culture

Legend has it that Rome was named after Romulus, who killed his brother Remus in order that the city bear his name. And therein lies the essence of the

Italian way of life: two brothers locked in mortal combat over a single vowel. Italians are a passionate but considerate people – passionate about what affects them and considerate of very little else. Like many capital cities, Rome is filled with people with an over-inflated sense of their own worth and any visitor is likely to encounter precocious and melodramatic behaviour on a level that you'd struggle to match even if you were to populate a city with Jennifer Lopez clones.

Conversation is conducted at two volumes in Rome – bellowing caterwaul for everyday exchanges and icy whisper for bitchy put-downs and romantic propositioning. Anything else is viewed as rude, as is being seen to eavesdrop on others' conversations, even when they're being conducted at eardrum-rupturing volumes. It's all too easy to see where Verdi drew his inspiration from once you've heard two Romans discussing who had the car keys last.

If people shouting tunelessly at each other in an over-the-top way is your thing though, then a trip to the Rome Opera House is something you should think about booking early in your trip. Rome's once-antiquated theatres are now beginning to abandon their obsession with bureaucracy and are fully computerised, making them much more efficient than they used to be. Forget about waiting for style-conscious but tardy postmen, who are more concerned about the wear and tear on their loafers than getting you your tickets in time. You can now book online quickly and easily and confirm your virtual tickets for the seats you didn't want for the wrong show in an instant.

Attractions

The centre of Rome is relatively small and can easily be crossed on foot, which is just as well, as you've got more chance of getting an audience with His Holiness Benedict XVI than you have of getting a parking permit from Rome's traffic police, who are clearly in denial that their empire either declined or

Before you know it you'll have had enough of the city and feel like escaping into the countryside that surrounds Rome. Like Sheffield, Rome is a city built on seven hills. But the similarities end there, for while Sheffield's hills are exposed and uninviting, the hills that surround Rome are desolate and windswept.

fell. Keep an eye out for the gangs of narcissistic bullyboys who loiter on street corners preening themselves, chatting up underage girls and generally looking for trouble – or the Carabinieri, as they're more properly known. These shaved gorillas have such a reputation for casual brutality that even other policemen avoid them.

The Coliseum and the giant wedding cake that is the Tomb of the Unknown Soldier are two of the many attractions that will guarantee you an added dash of local colour in the form of probably the world's most aggressive pickpockets. Your best bet is to secure any valuables, such as cameras or purses, around your neck and speed around as quickly as possible, stopping for nothing and no one. Forget about savouring the experience or soaking in the atmosphere of the place – just take pictures that you can enjoy at leisure in the comfort and security of your hotel room. Japanese tourists need not concern themselves with this travel tip, as this is what they do anyway.

Eating and Drinking

One of the great pleasures to be had from a trip to Rome is the food and drink, which is of a high standard throughout the city. Waiting staff are attentive and well trained and only very rarely forget to advise patrons that their home may be at risk if they cannot keep up repayments on their lunch.

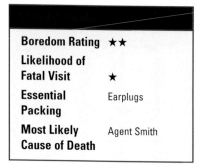

The birthplace of Mozart, where everything from chocolate bars and almond liqueur to haemorrhoid cream and home pregnancy-testing kits come bearing the composer's Don King-styled image.

Boredom Rating	★★
Likelihood of Fatal Visit	★
Essential Packing	Earplugs
Most Likely Cause of Death	Agent Smith

History

Austria experienced a period of remarkable stability for most of the last millennium, at least by the standards that Europe set for itself. The Habsburg dynasty enjoyed a lengthy reign from 1278 until the onset of World War I – which probably says more about the desirability of the region than the might of the dynasty. After such a lengthy period of abstinence from full-scale armed conflict, the nation state made sure it wasn't going to miss the last two great bashes of the 20th century, allowing a trivial little thing like the assassination of the Emperor's nephew to spark the flame that led to World War I and then embracing fascism like a long-lost brother who's just won the lottery at the advent of World War II. However, despite its somewhat shameful record and subsequent annexation in 1945, modern Austria has largely managed to shake off its reputation and consign the past to its history. In fact, the country has done such a good job of this that it seems to be suffering from collective amnesia – in the 2000 elections the right-wing Freedom Party came in second and maintain a controlling element in the country's parliament.

Culture

Salzburg has for centuries been considered one of the most picturesque cities in all of Europe, sheltered as it is by snow-capped mountains and centred around the clear blue water of the Salzach River. Many visitors become captivated by the charms of its manicured lawns, twee architecture and baroque plumbing. Such visitors are weak-willed fools who are failing to spot the obvious glitches in the *Matrix*.

Unsurprisingly, for a country so clearly in denial, the cultural emphasis is very much on the cloyingly sweet side. Focus on waltz music, alpine scenery and the chocolate coating on everything and you should forget the fact that in nearby Mauthausen Quarry the Nazis established a concentration camp and put prisoners to work on the notorious Stairway of Death. Admire the beauty of the old town nestled beneath the Hohensalzburg Fortress and don't think to ask how it escaped damage throughout World War II. If you're not into Mozart – and after three days anywhere in Austria you'll be sick of the sound of him – the only thing that Salzburg has going for it is that it's the one place on earth where *The Sound of Music* is loathed by everyone who's seen it. Not that that stops anyone from marketing tours based around the locations used in that piece of filmic torture.

Attractions

The Salzburg Festival runs from late July until the end of August. It celebrates all things Austrian and should therefore be avoided at all costs. October 26th is National Day, when the fiercely patriotic natives of Salzburg take to the streets for more flag waving than you'll see anywhere else in Europe – fortunately with a lot less goose-stepping than used to be the case.

Eating and Drinking

Austria's cuisine is an interesting fusion of old-style stodge and nouvelle starch. There's something for everyone not on the Atkins Diet, and nothing at all for those who are. Carb-avoiders will be going home hungry – and, as a result, the envy of all their friends who did get to eat.

One of the most striking things for the Western visitor is the relaxed attitude to underage drinking. Bartenders, shopkeepers and McDonalds staff are all more than happy to serve alcohol to anyone, regardless of age, appearance or provision of ID. This presents no problem to the über-disciplined youth of the city, who are far too focussed on their skiing, psychedelic beanie hats and *glockenspiel* practice to indulge in the 80-percent-proof Stroh Inlander rum that fuels the truck drivers, high-school teachers and traffic cops. However, it's an absolute nightmare once you introduce teenage Brits and Yanks into the mix. Evidence of these off-the-leash reprobates enjoying their first beer is to be found in the pavement pizzas dotted all over the old town's quaint cobblestones.

A popular choice – for people ordering Austrian food for the first time, at least – is *wiener schnitzel*. A mystery meat – often veal – deep fried and coated in egg, breadcrumbs, raisins and cinnamon. Those who find the idea of veal repugnant may be comforted to discover that the calves are not killed purely for their sweet young flesh. Their innards also have their part to play in Austrian cuisine, such as in *beuschel*, a tasty treat made from thin slices of the cute infant's heart and lungs.

Once you've finished your dinner, you'll no doubt be keen to wolf down a traditional Austrian dessert – or indeed anything at all that will take away the taste of your traditional Austrian main course. *Salzburger nockerl* is a soufflé that's every bit as enticing as its name suggests, leaving a metallic aftertaste in the mouth and sitting in your stomach for the rest of your stay like an unexploded limpet mine. Shout "*Schmanker*" at your waiter and he'll wheel up the sweet trolley. You'll probably feel like shouting something very similar at him after one bite of his recommendation.

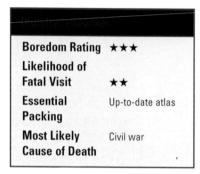

Travellers planning to arrive in Skopje by road should be aware that no matter how up-to-date they think their maps are, they should approach crossing points with caution, as Macedonia changes its borders more often than Jennifer Lopez changes her husband.

Boredom Rating	★★★
Likelihood of Fatal Visit	★★
Essential Packing	Up-to-date atlas
Most Likely Cause of Death	Civil war

History

In 1898, Bismarck said that if there was ever to be another war in Europe, it would come out of some damn silly thing in the Balkans. And how right he was, providing you don't count trifling little skirmishes in Romania, Poland, Cyprus, Russia, Czechoslovakia, Poland, Greece, Spain and of course the two World Wars, one of which he helped start.

Macedonia was historically a part of Greece and a large settlement of Slav tribes in the seventh century sowed the seeds of its remarkable history. The region changed hands like a bad penny for a thousand years or so until an uprising against Turkish rule in the early 20th century gave Macedonia a nationalist leader, Goce Delcev, who was martyred in the name of independence. A series of wars fought by Greece, Serbia, Bulgaria and Turkey led to Macedonia's nationalist cause being advanced not at all, and the region was divided and even managed to lose the right to use its own name.

The success of Yugoslavian folk hero Tito's partisans in World War II – many of whom were Macedonian – led to a recognition of the region and the ultimate granting of independence in 1992. At which point things started to get really interesting, as an apparently peaceful process became complicated by

Greek claims to having copyright on the name Macedonia, Albanian separatists asking if it was OK for them to have independence too, and the arrival of 1,000 UN troops with as much understanding of the political situation in the region as President Clinton has of what constituted "sexual relations".

Culture

As you might expect from a country with such a confused identity, Macedonia has a diverse culture. The good news is that wherever you go, it's consistently bad. Whether the *Greatest Hits of Fleetwood Mac* are being murdered on lute and bagpipes by Bulgarians, Albanians, Slavs, Greeks or any of the other confusing ethnic divisions within this remarkable country, you know you're listening to music you'll never want to hear again.

Attractions

Devastated by an earthquake in 1963 that claimed more than 1,000 lives, Skopje is a city of remarkable contrasts. Aid money poured into the region in the wake of the disaster and city planners set about planning the city's rebirth with all the detail and finesse of a three-year-old given crayons for the first time. As a result, Skopje may be the only city on earth where you won't need to ask directions to get to the post office – it's the big ugly complex that casts a

The most popular dance in Macedonia is an all-male affair that starts slow, gets frantic and rather worryingly is known as *Teskoto*, or "the Hard One". Said to symbolise the awakening of the desire for national independence, it's all too easy to see how it can also be seen as an allegory for a whole host of other kinds of awakening desires.

shadow over everything. The city also features several structures that date back to the 15th century, notably the stone bridge that spans the Vardar and the domed Daud Pasha, once a Turkish Bath and now a notably art-free art gallery. Both of these look likely to be standing long after anything built in the last 30 years.

Eating and Drinking

Follow your nose and you'll find traditional grilled mincemeat for sale. Apparently it's traditional not to tell visitors what it was that actually got minced to provide you with lunch, so if you're in any doubt, try the *ohrid* trout, which is exactly as it sounds.

Slough

Just because somewhere is universally derided doesn't necessarily mean it's to be avoided…or does it?

Facts and Figures	
Boredom Rating	★★★★★
Likelihood of Fatal Visit	★
Essential Packing	Complete set of The Office on DVD
Most Likely Cause of Death	Overexposure

History

Nestling in the county of Berkshire a short jaunt from London just off the M25 motorway (one of the most accomplished feats in modern civil engineering) and the internationally famous Pinewood Studios lies Slough, a town so bereft of anything interesting it very nearly belies belief. Named after a patch of muddy land between the bustling towns of Upton and Eton, Slough pretty much represents everything that has gone wrong with Great Britain since it decided it didn't really want to be a part of Europe after all and instead tried to model its development on that of the US. The population of the area, which was a trading estate in the 1920s, swelled from a night-watchman and his two dogs to nearly 30,000 after World War II, when housing estates were built at nearby Britwell and Langley to accommodate Londoners desperate to escape the threat of continual cockney knees-up singalongs. Today its population is around 120,000, all of whom would much rather be somewhere else.

Culture

Slough is notable for looking like just about every other small-to-medium-size town in Great Britain, only a bit worse. A combination of short-sighted town planning, local-authority ineptitude, central-government indifference and multinational-corporation dominance have meant that the majority of local shops, small businesses, independent craftsmen and people with any sense of good taste have long since abandoned the area. What has replaced them is the jumble of faux-Americana, Euro-homogenisation and plucky British Bulldog mainstay (funded and operated by French, German or Japanese management companies) to be found on most British high streets, albeit in a slightly different order – though not so much that you'd actually notice.

Attractions

A trip to the Queensmere Shopping Centre is about as good as it gets in Slough, and also tells you all you need to know about the town itself. Like the American post-war boom-town developments, both the town of Slough and the Queensmere complex were an attempt to carve a little bit of the American Dream out in a corner of Berkshire for a few lucky Brits. The trouble is that the American Dream only really applies to America, a country with a diverse culture, a wild and varied landscape and, above all, a lot of space. About ten million square kilometres of it. Take the American Dream and try applying it anywhere else in the world and you get Slough – and more particularly you get the Queensmere Shopping Centre. Not any kind of dream, just a poky little nightmare that's a graveyard of vacant outlets populated by glue-sniffing teens with dreams of one day making it as far as Reading.

How Not to Slough
Should you have the misfortune to spend an evening here, Slough has several theatre companies, none of which is professional. If your tastes extend as far as seeing actors who aren't market researchers or sex-line chat girls by day, you could go to the Theatre Royal in nearby Windsor, though the constant gridlock of tourists flocking to take photos of the royal bolthole there makes it a journey rarely worth the effort.

John Betjeman was ahead of his time when he wrote: "Come friendly bombs and fall on Slough."

Eating and Drinking

The restaurants in Slough may not be of a high standard, but they are fairly cheap, particularly if you choose to "go large" for an extra 30p. Drinking is advised before you go, during your stay and long after you've left if you ever hope to forget the dreadful experience.

After a difficult period establishing itself as a national state, independent of the former USSR, Bulgaria recently shot to the top of the world production league tables for static electricity, an achievement that can be put down to the population's preference for man-made fibres.

Boredom Rating	★★★★
Likelihood of Fatal Visit	★★
Essential Packing	Breath mints
Most Likely Cause of Death	Drunk driver in charge of car, bus, train or donkey and cart

History

Bulgarian history is as rich in patriotic heroism as it is in utter stupidity, which is truly saying something. Since the Russians liberated it from Turkish rule in 1878 it has modelled itself as an annoying little brother to the Soviet super state, sharing close ties with it while occasionally showing its independence as if to prove it is no mere satellite. This kind of outside-the-box thinking has got the country where it is today, veering from monarchy to republic and back again and leading the Bulgarian Army to issue its troops with the world's first reversible military fatigues during World War II in order to save time and money whenever they changed sides. The collapse of communism has given Bulgaria the chance to forge a new identity, an opportunity it has wasted no time in resolutely ignoring.

Culture

Architecturally, Sofia is remarkably diverse, with post-war concrete atrocities nestling dejectedly alongside older buildings so ugly the Nazis couldn't even be bothered to raze them to the ground. The whole dizzy mix is tied mercilessly together by a yellow brick boulevard, which actually started life as a white brick boulevard but has been stained over the years by a generations of hard-drinking Bulgarians caught short between licensed premises.

Attractions

While it may be struggling to find its economic feet since the iron curtain rusted and fell off the map, Bulgaria does lead the world in arcane and bizarre public-holiday celebrations. For example, while the rest of the planet celebrates Valentine's Day, Bulgarians devote February 14th to *Trifon Zarezan* – the ancient festival of the wine growers. Like most Bulgarian festivals, this involves a couple of minutes of random activity in meaningless costume followed by 12–14 hours of hard drinking.

Folk music is extremely popular in Bulgaria and Sofia's folk clubs fill up quickly with folkies, drinkers and masochists eager to soak up extended sets into the early hours of the morning or until their livers collapse, whichever comes first.

Eating and Drinking

Ask any Bulgarian man in the street if food and drink are important to him and he'll reply *"Da!"* Ask him what his favourite food is and he'll say *"Da!"* again, and you'll notice for the first time that he seems to be staggering slightly. He'll then ask you to repeat the question before declaring you his best friend in the

Mount Vitosha lies just to the south of Sofia and forms part of the mountainous landscape that borders the country and that has played a crucial role in deterring potential invaders – though it would be only fair to point out that as deterrents go there is little to beat the less-than-gentle strains of traditional Bulgarian folk music.

world and falling over. Bulgarians live as much of their lives as possible in a state of inebriation, which is not surprising given their cheerless surroundings and the ready availability of high-strength spirits from shops, street traders and nursery-school staff. As a result, cooking has become a less and less important facet of the culture, as Bulgarians spend most of their waking hours too pissed to realise that they're even hungry. This can present troubles for visitors to the country looking to eat out as the act of eating is now viewed as behaviour that's at best eccentric and at worst suspicious. Your best bet may be to adopt the host culture for the duration of the stay and aim to be plastered by 11am. However, if you should choose to, you can follow the yellow-brick boulevard into the town centre where you'll find the very best that Bulgarian cuisine has to offer – a new Subway franchise.

St Tropez

Playground of the rich, famous, leathery skinned and those far too old to be wearing a thong. Not that that stops them.

Boredom Rating	★★★
Likelihood of Fatal Visit	★
Essential Packing	Anti-nausea tablets
Most Likely Cause of Death	Skin cancer

History

Like far too many places in France, St. Tropez was probably once a charming little hamlet with friendly locals, beautiful views and a peaceful, unhurried atmosphere. Then it was discovered by the rest of the world, and it's been hurtling downhill ever since.

Nestled on the Côte d'Azur between Hyères and St. Maxime – two beautiful towns that offer all of the benefits of the Riviera for half the money and next to no hassle – St. Tropez has for most of its history been just another seaport on the south coast of France. Things began to shift after the harbour, destroyed during World War II, was rebuilt, and in the early '50s the town became a popular summer resort for creative types from Paris looking to escape the tourist crush of their home city in the summer. Sadly, they weren't capable of being discreet about it, and

by the time that Brigitte Bardot began enticing the rest of the world to come enjoy its delights, St. Tropez was already the worst-kept celebrity retreat secret in the world.

Culture

The French have a reputation for philosophy, introspection and deep thought that is well earned – but entirely absent from any aspect of life in St. Tropez, a town that values everything by how it looks on the surface. This is unfortunate, since while there are admittedly beautiful people to be seen in St. Tropez, they rarely travel in pairs. This severely restricts the fun to be had from grabbing an outside table at a café (after a three-hour wait) and doing some serious people watching over a glass or four of *Pastis*. That 19-year-old in the electric-mauve bikini may well have the body of a *Playboy* centrefold, but your appreciation of her is likely to be seriously undermined by the presence next to her of a guy who could easily pass for Danny DeVito's less-attractive older brother if he gave his back a shave. And similarly, there are himbos with abs you could bevel furniture with, but unless they're all devoted grandsons taking grandma out for a bodysurfing lesson it's probably safe for you to assume that they're being paid by the hour for catering to the needs of their elderly charges. And it's probably best not to even think about what they get paid for doing the rest of the time.

Where you'll choose to eat and drink

St. Tropez will hit your pocket hard, so head to Place aux Herbes for the fruit and vegetable market, which takes place three times a week. In line with the town's new unwelcoming approach to tourists, most traders are unwilling to sell anything to anyone from out of town. However, if you look pained enough, you might be able to get lucky with one of them. Failing that, you could always scavenge the floor to see if you can find enough discarded produce to keep yourself alive.

Attractions

While St. Tropez made its name as a resort catering to the needs of celebrities, you're about as likely to run into a superstar there as you are to avoid a five-mile tailback of traffic on the road in. Brigitte Bardot may have sent out the invitations for what was once the ultimate party town, but she's spent the last few years trying to convince everyone that the fun's over and it's time to go home. Any celebrities you see are likely to be k-list at best.

Place des Lices is not a termite colony but a plane-tree-lined square where such wannabes gather for games of petanque and the opportunity to show off their *Miami Vice*-inspired outfits. In the unlikely event of anyone famous arriving in town, rest assured that a waiting helicopter, an army of bodyguards and a curtained-off VIP area in whatever restaurant you were lucky enough to bribe your way into will ensure you get no closer to their divinity than the back row of paparazzi.

Eating and Drinking

Chez Joseph and Chez Maggi are both reasonably priced by Riviera standards, and therefore totally out of the price range of most mere mortals.

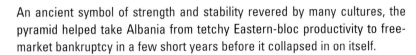

Tirana

An ancient symbol of strength and stability revered by many cultures, the pyramid helped take Albania from tetchy Eastern-bloc productivity to free-market bankruptcy in a few short years before it collapsed in on itself.

Country: Albania	
Boredom Rating	★★★★★
Likelihood of Fatal Visit	★★
Essential Packing	Pen and paper (for writing home when telephone network collapses)
Most Likely Cause of Death	Organ-donation pyramid scheme

History

All too often a short-stay parking bay for conquering armies looking to pick up a few souvenirs in Greece, Albania has in its time been occupied by Romans, Slavs, Huns, Serbians, French, Italians, Austro-Hungarians, Ostrogoths, Visigoths and common or garden Goths during The Jesus and Mary Chain's last European tour. The only East European state to succeed in kicking out the Nazis during World War II without the aid of Soviet forces, it allied itself to Stalin and resisted the West's efforts to put it back on the path of democracy and openness via the traditional means of secret-service-sponsored insurrection. Having got itself firmly into Mother Russia's good books, Albania then spent the next 20 years pissing her off, refusing to let Khrushchev play with his submarines off the coast in 1960 and then breaking it off with the Warsaw Pact in 1968 because it wanted an open relationship.

The collapse of communism brought demonstrations, the introduction of opposition parties and an abandonment of the central planning that had governed the Albanian economy in favour of a free-market approach, largely through the growth of extensive pyramid schemes. Optimistic predictions by the UN on the country's economic future in the early '90s served inevitably as a kiss of death for its fragile confidence and led it up the financial creek, where it currently finds itself adrift without a paddle. The one area of private enterprise that certainly seems to be on the rise is bargain-basement European tours – or "human trafficking" as it's more commonly called. If you drive into Tirana, it's worth checking the boot of your car before you depart.

Culture

Despite a depressing economic outlook, the people of Albania remain irrepressibly cheerful and have not only sought to keep old cultural traditions alive, but have also originated many new schools of artistic expression. Disillusionment is now a recognised art form, which is eligible for cash grants from the government. Polyphony – the blending of numerous vocal or instrumental parts – is prevalent throughout Tirana, most notably from drivers capable of

An addiction to Norman Wisdom films has also led to a high demand for crepe.

Albanian Countryside

Get out of the city and explore one of the once-beautiful national forests that are a short drive from Tirana. These were once dense and not navigable on foot, but since becoming the prime fuel supply for the country they are a lot easier to get around.

combining the strains of over-revved 800cc engines with vocal remonstrations and incessant horn blaring, while precariously leaning out of the passenger-seat window. It's worth remembering that Albanians drive on the other side of the road at all times. Lastly, Albania is one of the few countries in the world where Norman Wisdom is still revered as an international film great. While most Britons grew up cursing the black and white films they were made to watch on wet Sunday afternoons, the Albanians took the little chancer to their hearts.

Attractions

Skenderberg Square, a meeting point for the city's legions of refugee smugglers and counterfeiters, is the gaping wound at the heart of Tirana. It was designed to accommodate the kind of military parade of tanks and rocket launchers that the Albanian government aspired to before they lost the tanks and rocket launchers, along with all the guns and soldiers, in the aftermath of the pyramid-scheme collapse. Bear in mind that jaywalking anywhere in the city is an offence punishable by a fine – which will be payable by your family in the likely event of your death – and that it is all too easy to be uncertain where the pavement ends and the road begins, particularly if you are an Albanian driver.

Eating and Drinking

Economic decline has driven many of Tirana's restaurants into receivership, so your best bet is to ask your hotel to prepare you a picnic and head out of the city. Spread your *Militia Albania* ("property of the Albanian Army") blanket on one of the many concrete pillboxes that litter the countryside. Albanian food is Turkish influenced and dominated by meat – though no one seems too sure about what meat exactly. Avoid picnicking near any of Albania's rivers, as an organic approach to sewage treatment (i.e. not treating it) is liable to put you off your lunch, assuming its contents haven't done that already.

Most of Tirana's government buildings are based on designs seen in episodes of *Thunderbirds* and *Stingray*. Sadly, Tirana's communications HQ, "Marineville", does not slide underground in emergencies.

LET'S NOT GO TO...

The Middle East

EXPECT TO HEAR SOMEONE SHOUTING AT YOU:
"Go home, Western dogs! But buy a carpet first."

MOST OBVIOUS LOW POINTS:
The Dead Sea

SLIGHT COMPENSATIONS:
Dates are very cheap

OVERALL RATING: ★

★★★★★	**KINGDOM OF HEAVEN**
★★★★	**ROCK THE KASBAH**
★★★	**SALAAM BAM THANK YOU MA'AM**
★★	**MOUSTACHE RUMBLE**
★	**1001 NIGHTMARES**

Beirut

Beirut's reputation as the Paris of the Middle East is well earned – unfortunately the Paris in question is the Nazi-occupied city of 1940–4.

Country: Lebanon	
Boredom Rating ★	
Likelihood of Fatal Visit	★★★
Essential Packing	American flag and good-quality matches
Most Likely Cause of Death	Mortar fire

History

In Biblical times, Lebanon was said to be a land of milk and honey. Far from delighting in this label, the hapless Lebanese have been trying to ditch it ever since. The prospect of easy pickings has led every freebooting nation on earth to pay a visit, meaning that Beirut has been consistently ravaged for as long as anyone can remember. Given the predominance of shell-shock among the inhabitants, this, though, is never very long. The Phoenicians,

The Dead Sea

The Dead Sea has been making non-swimmers feel good about themselves for thousands of years – and making the rest of us question why anyone on earth would want to come on a beach holiday here. The high density of mineral salts means that while you need not pack a lilo, the life expectancy of any plant or fish that finds itself in the Dead Sea is low even by Beirut's standards. The Dead Sea is truly a must-see for anyone who hates the ocean. For everyone else, the best thing to be said about it is that it is sinking 13 inches a year and so hopefully won't be with us for all that much longer.

Assyrians, Neo-Babylonians, Persians and Romans all got their piece of the Lebanese pie before the rise of the first great Muslim dynasty led to almost a century of relative stability in the seventh century AD. Then things got really complicated.

In the last century, European involvement in the region benefited Lebanon in the same way that lead weights help a drowning man, though, on a positive note, the horror of the internecine struggles of the last 100 years has meant that invading armies have become a thing of the past. Even the most hardened of dictators would blanch at the thought of occupying a country where civil war has become the national pastime. Armed militia groups head for Beirut like wannabe starlets head for Hollywood, and while they prefer to use the majority of time (and ammunition) on each other, it's all too easy to get caught in the

The local council provides telephones, electricity and hotline access points. Sewerage is planned for 2014.

When booking your hotel room, remember to ask if it comes with a balcony.

crossfire. This is especially true should you be unfortunate enough to encounter one of the new radical groups whose martyr-like determination to cause death and destruction has been attributed to them being pissed off that all the good three-letter names (PLO, LSF) have already been taken. Armed factions are listed in the Beirut press like share prices and outnumber piles of rubble in a city .

Culture

Whatever else may be said about the Middle East, it is clearly a part of the world rich in culture. More than 71 percent of the world's ancient wonders are to be found here. Admittedly, 89 percent of those wonders are less than 20 percent intact, but nonetheless the ruins are always very nicely arranged. Many such historical sites are located a short drive from Beirut – such as the Temple of Bacchus in Baalbek. And if ruins are your thing, there's every chance that by the time you've

made it through the roadblocks and back into the city, that's exactly the state you'll find your hotel in.

Attractions

Pigeon Rocks are probably the most famous natural feature of Beirut. These offshore rock arches are a lovely complement to Beirut's dramatic sea cliffs, and local couples are often to be seen taking a romantic stroll along the Corniche, Beirut's coastal road, to watch the sunset there, take in the sea air and discharge small arms fire at the circling seagulls.

Eating and Drinking

Lebanese cuisine is an exciting fusion of Turkish and Arabic cooking given a French spin to produce results unlike anything you'll ever want to taste again. The best time for gourmets to sample the delights of Beirut cuisine is during the festival of Ramadan, when all restaurants are closed all day.

Bethlehem

And so it came to pass that Christ was born of Mary and did walk the Earth, preaching a creed of generosity, pacifism and non-materialism. And, lo, since that day, squabbling, armed conflict and horrendous overcharging for parking have plagued the lands on which he walked.

Country: Palestine	
Boredom Rating	★★
Likelihood of Fatal Visit	★★
Essential Packing	Little donkey
Most Likely Cause of Death	Joining a queue

History

Target of more holy campaigns than Salman Rushdie and Marilyn Manson combined, the Holy Land has been claimed in the name of an all-powerful but forgiving god any number of times, usually by a marauding army of vicious thugs whose second act was to organise schedules for looting, raping and temple-sacking.

With antagonism between Islam and Judaism on the rise by the end of the 19th century, Britain did the best it could with its mandate to rule Israel after World War I by proposing a compromise solution. Having come up with proposals for an Arab state with a Jewish homeland that left both sides even more unhappy than they had been before the stupid compromise, Britain was glad to then wash its hands of the situation. Since then, Palestine has experienced some brief, but nonetheless colourful, wars and endured ceasefires made so noisy by men discharging weapons into the air that everyone just assumes it's time to start fighting again.

Culture

With more religion packed into every square inch than any small town could handle, the preachers struggle to be heard in Bethlehem. As a result they tend to shout rather a lot. Chapel time is strictly rationed between faiths, with Greek Orthodox, Armenian and Roman Catholic all doing their best to overrun on their sermons and eat into each other's time. If you've come to Bethlehem on a spiritual pilgrimage, it may be worth your while taking in a service by another denomination if you're headed for one of the major chapels. You may disagree with what they're preaching with every fibre in your soul, but at least you're guaranteed a seat when your guys make it to the altar.

Attractions

Most people come to Bethlehem in search of answers. What questions you are likely to find the answers to in such a rundown suburb is anyone's guess, but the town planners are certainly aware of the mythic power of a name and do their best to play up to the Christmas-spirit expectations of the cattle loads of arriving tourists with road names such as Shepherd's Street, Manger Place and Nintendo Avenue. The centrepiece of Bethlehem's majesty, Manger Square, is a car park. Not that you'll be able to park your car here. Consider yourself lucky if you've managed to negotiate your way past enough checkpoints to be able to see Manger Square from your vehicle. Abandon your rental car and ask directions for the Church of the Nativity before

Diving in Israel

The coast of Israel offers some excellent opportunities for diving these days – and unlike in the Gaza Strip, it won't just be for cover. If you are a serious diver, remember to do anything necessary to ensure you don't get an Israeli stamp in your passport, as this will restrict your ability to travel just about anywhere else in the Middle East.

Don't expect the, "How still we see thee lie" Bethlehem of the carol. And you'll have to look very hard to find three wise men.

heading in the opposite direction – that is unless your idea of a good time is watching the back of someone else's head for a couple of hours while you're jostled from every side by perspiring Bible-bashing families from Delaware. The over-crowding is worst at Christmas, and for six months either side of it.

Eating and Drinking

With the situation in Palestine being what it is, it's nice to find something that both sides are clearly agreed on: asking for a bacon sandwich in Bethlehem is unlikely to be met with any success.

Cairo

With attractions that are showing their age after 4,500 years and a human-rights record that makes it a favoured spot for US military interrogations, Cairo has less to recommend it as each grain of sand trickles through the hourglass.

Country: Egypt	
Boredom Rating	★
Likelihood of Fatal Visit	★★★
Essential Packing	Pocket calculator
Most Likely Cause of Death	Over-enthusiastic haggling

Though the authorities accept that there are many marginal relationships in modern Egypt, they are still not sanctioned by the state.

History

A civilisation that dates back 6,000 years but that is still struggling with such basic concepts as air-conditioning installation and underarm deodorant, Egypt is home to nearly 17 million people, 16,999, 950 of whom will seem to be within arm's length from the moment you arrive until you gratefully depart. Cairo is, of course, famous for being home to some remarkable remains of an ancient civilisation, which have been kept well preserved by the region's dry desert climate. Sadly, Cairo has been a popular destination for empire-building nations for as long as Egyptians have taken such a grand approach to crypt building, so many sites have been vandalised by those keen to improve later generations' appreciation of the wonders on show by carving messages, their own names and impromptu games of noughts and crosses into the ancient masonry.

A swampy backwater until the mid-19th century, modern Cairo was designed in a European style by the French-educated premier Ismail and financed by a succession of European banks, who matched the creative vision of the planners and architects with spectacular interest rates. Faced with spiralling repayments, it was only a matter of time before the bailiffs were called in. The Brits, however, were considerate enough to let building work be completed on the commercially and strategically

The Riddled Face of The Sphinx

Seeing the Sphinx is always a shock for Westerners who'd just assumed that the reason she looked so blurry on the TV was the travel show producer blocking out a sponsor's logo on her nose. But no, she really does look that bad. Recent restoration attempts have actually accelerated the rate of decay, giving her all the mythic beauty of Juliette Wildenstein fresh out of surgery after her most recent cosmetic procedure.

vital Suez canal before sending in the army to take control of it, and everything else in Egypt, in 1882.

Culture

After successfully throwing off the shackles of colonial oppression in the revolution of 1952, the city of Cairo set about re-inventing itself as a truly modern Egyptian city, which is evident in the layout and design of the ugly sprawling suburbs that now surround the old city. Medinat Nasr, Medinat Mohandiseen and the Muqattam Hills developments are all characterised by up-to-the minute design, providing the minute you're talking about is the one that occurred some time in the late '50s when the International Convention of Architects and Town Planners named cheap poured concrete as the "building material of the future". While it could be argued that the grimness of the modern architecture serves as a startling counterpoint to the majesty of the Pyramids, this too is changing as the effects of pollution, overcrowding and overuse of flash photography continue to transform Cairo into a collection of bizarre crumbling buildings.

Attractions

Of all the world's seven wonders, only the Pyramids at Giza are still standing, which is more than can be said for most of the construction that has gone on in Cairo in the last few years. Entry to the site is free, but industrious and unofficial "temple guards" will charge to let you climb up the inside, or to head into a darkened chamber to see collections of mummified hands up close. Guards will also often charge to let you leave a site, and it is generally best not to argue with them about this, unless you want to find out for yourself where they've been getting all their mummified hands from.

Eating and Drinking

Cairo has many restaurants that cater to every kind of budget. However, travellers are advised not to shell out too much on dinner, since whatever you choose to eat will only have time to make a passing acquaintance with your stomach before continuing it's progress through your digestive system and out the other end within the hour.

A rug worker tries in vain to cross the magic carpet picket line

Damascus

Given the state of what's at the end of it, theologians are increasingly of the opinion that any conversions experienced on the Road to Damascus are merely lame excuses designed to avoid completing the trip.

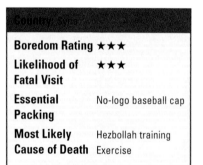

Country: Syria

Boredom Rating	★★★
Likelihood of Fatal Visit	★★★
Essential Packing	No-logo baseball cap
Most Likely Cause of Death	Hezbollah training Exercise

History

The capital of the Muslim world for as long as the Islamic *Umayyads* had anything to do with it, and home to one of the oldest civilisations in the world, Syria has been granted only the briefest of periods of independence in its long, turbulent history. And judging by what it's chosen to do with itself given the opportunity, it's no wonder the rest of the planet has been so determined to keep a firm grip on it.

The fuzziness of the region's frontiers and competing influences from French, British and American

Starbucks recently chose the city to test market its new chain of walking coffee shops.

expeditionary forces meant it entered the 20th century unsure of its own identity. It took two World Wars for its diverse population to find an idea they could unite behind – getting rid of their French overlords – and at that point modern Syria was born.

Civilian rule proved unpopular – with the military at least – and armed coups became the rage, culminating in the rise to power of former night fighter-pilot Hafiz Assad, who cultivated links with the USSR, which ensured they remained one of the most tooled-up states in the Middle East. When Soviet stock waned, Syria got on the anti-Iraq bandwagon in an attempt to get into America's good books – something that was unlikely to happen as long as Hezbollah remained the number-one state-sponsored organisation.

Culture

Muslim, Roman and Byzantine ruins are everywhere in Damascus, though they're in such an advanced stage of disrepair that Indiana Jones would have trouble telling them apart. Syrians are very hospitable and you can expect to be invited off the street for a cup of tea by anyone with whom you exchange eye contact. This will allow you to get a real feel for Syrian life, and allow Syrian muggers to do their business out of sight of the ever-watchful police.

Attractions

The major attraction to Damascus for the original settlers was the convergence of the Barada River and the Ghouta Oasis, the only things that made the otherwise barren region inhabitable. But why anyone would choose to make the trek to Damascus now is a mystery to everyone, residents of the city included.

Eating and Drinking

Food in Damascus is among the best you'll find in the Middle East. So you'd better make sure you don't arrive there during the month-long festival of Ramadan unless you're looking to lose a few pounds.

Fallujah

Only aid workers, visiting dignitaries and military personnel are currently being allowed into Iraq. So, the international community has got it one-third right.

Country: Iraq

Boredom Rating	★
Likelihood of Fatal Visit	★★★★★
Essential Packing	Soldier of Fortune magazine
Most Likely Cause of Death	Correct. Your death is likely to be in the name of a cause. Who knows which.

History

From the Black Sheep Turkmen tribe of the 14th century to black sheep of the international community by the end of the 20th, Iraq's passage through history has been as bloody as a trainee drug mule's misguided attempt to smuggle a consignment of razor blades. Created from the lumping together of the three provinces of Mosul, Baghdad and Basra by the British in the aftermath of World War I, Iraq was given a monarchy, a constituent assembly and a visit from Winston Churchill, then colonial secretary.

It became clear during the assembly's first debate, on the choice of fabric and colour for the parliament building's entrance hall, that the framework established by the British was intrinsically unstable and liable to promote insurrection, paranoia, coups and countercoups. Happy with their work, the British agreed to Iraqi calls for independence and wasted no time in getting the hell out, and since 1932 Iraq has been getting itself into trouble without outside help from anyone. War with Israel, Iran, Kurdistan and everyone on the planet who jumped on the bandwagon to save poor little oil-rich Kuwait helped the country rack up debts as high as Elton John's hair-transplant bills, and sanctions and trade embargoes have left it with a population as malnourished and sickly as a limo full of supermodels.

Culture

A constant diet of oppression, gunfire, summary imprisonment without trial and state-of-the art torture has put the people of Iraq on the ropes. And that's just since the Americans arrived in town. Prior to that, things were even worse. Terrorised by a CIA-sponsored tyrant and his barmy family, bombed to bits by mistake and design, held responsible by association for 9/11 and accused of having WMDs at a time when the army was struggling to issue all of its men with laces for their boots, Iraq is as unlucky a country as exists in the world today, and Fallujah is the epicentre of its misery. The good news for travellers is that the only new arrivals in Fallujah at the moment are hapless babies on the downside of the Karmic cycle.

Attractions

The most violence-prone town in the most war-torn country on earth has little to recommend it to anyone interested in seeing another day – but this is

I Like Working for Uncle Sam

New intake is a key requirement of the United States Marine Corps, who have played a vital role in policing Fallujah. Their recruiting slogan, "Nobody likes to fight, but someone has to know how", was recently dropped, however, after it became clear that most Marines did like to fight, even if they didn't always know how, and were having a particularly hard time getting the hang of the laser targeting for their Tomahawk Missiles.

The road to the second Fallujah siege and walk was surprisingly quiet

precisely what has recommended it to the only individuals allowed entry to the country independent of any aid, military or diplomatic organisation. Mercenaries can expect to earn up to $5,000 a month for taking up security roles in Iraq, and the lack of entertainment offered by the Muslim host culture has given them time to organise the country's first National Bare-Knuckle Fighting, Handcuffed Arm Wrestling and Holding Your Breath Underwater Triathlon, which the citizens of Fallujah have jumped at the chance to compete in heats for.

Eating and Drinking

With the UN Food for Oil programme lying in tatters in the dust just next to Kofi Annan's reputation, your best bet for eating anything is winning MREs from the resident troops in a game of Hold 'em. The MRE (Meal Ready to Eat) provides an average of 1,250 kilocalories, requires no preparation and can last for three years at room temperature or up to five years with cold storage. Sounds tempting, huh?

Kabul

The capital of Afghanistan was never a terribly attractive or interesting city, something that has certainly not improved during the last 20 years of conflict.

Country: Afghanistan	
Boredom Rating	★★★★
Likelihood of Fatal Visit	★★★★★
Essential Packing	FBI most-wanted roster
Most Likely Cause of Death	Talking to the wrong woman (any woman)

History

Famous for it's uniformly brown, semi-razed architecture and radical approach to women's rights, Kabul is situated at an elevation of 1800m, making it one of the highest capital cities in the world – though this in itself is no good reason to visit. The nation's chief economic and cultural centre, rivalled only by a small shoe repair and key-cutting shop three miles to the north, it has long been of strategic importance because of it's proximity to the Khyber Pass, an important mountain route which currently allows goats to travel freely between Afghanistan and Pakistan. This perhaps explains why armies throughout history have sought to occupy Kabul. In the last century British, Soviet and American forces have all had a go at policing the region with mixed levels of success, ranging from completely disastrous to utterly catastrophic. Throughout all of this the people of Afghanistan have remained as positive as ever, largely thanks to their naturally resilient nature.

The city's many Georgian-style crescents have been given a dramatic new look by UN Forces

And the bandits, drug runners and Taliban guerrilla fighters have remained as capable of causing mayhem and widespread destruction as ever, thanks largely to the CIA for supplying them with state-of-the-art weaponry for fifteen years or so.

Culture

Despite invasion and occupation, many elements of Kabul's cultural heritage are in extremely good condition, usually in the private collections of the sponsors of the country's prosperous looting industry. This makes visiting Kabul's museums about as interesting as a stroll around an empty warehouse. But whilst what remains in Kabul are only the remnants of a once proud artistic and architectural legacy, at least those remnants are now preserved safely for future generations. In most cases by a thick layer of exploded plaster, crumbled masonry and dead bodies.

Attractions

Despite chronic under-funding, insufficient sign-posting and a multi-storey car-park that's accessible only via an Apache airlift, Kabul Zoo remains the number one tourist attraction in the city. In particular, the lion enclosure has won plaudits worldwide. This is due in part to its sympathetic design, which closely replicates the natural habitat of its big cats. But credit must also go to erratic US satellite-navigation technology, which has meant that for the last five years the lions have been kept well nourished on a diet of misdirected US paratroops.

Eating and Drinking

Any commercial transaction in Kabul has to include displaying a valid travel visa bearing the country's stamp, an icon of a poppy growing out of two piles of rubble. A visa is therefore essential to anyone wishing to spend an evening in one of Kabul's many restaurants, or at least it would be if any of Kabul's restaurants were still open, or indeed standing. Still, the visa will at least entitle you to queue up for a Red Cross food parcel.

Riyadh

Riyadh is not the place to go out on the lash. Unless you don't mind going under it the next day.

Country: Saudi Arabia	
Boredom Rating	★★★
Likelihood of Fatal Visit	★★
Essential Packing	Antiseptic cream
Most Likely Cause of Death	You'd rather not know

History

Saudi Arabia effectively came into being in the early 18th century, when the Al-Saud family formed an alliance with Mohammed bin Abdul Wahab and came up with a new improved interpretation of Islam that, backed by a some fairly aggressive canvassing, swept through the region as far as southern Iraq and remains the country's official religion.

The discovery of oil in 1938 ushered in an era of construction, prosperity and outside interest from Western leaders wanting to suck up to the Saudi Royal family and Middle Eastern leaders wanting their own piece of the pie. Today, Saudi Arabia is between the proverbial rock and hard place – despite withdrawal of American military personnel who missed the memo about the Gulf War being over, it's still seen as an ally of Bush in a part of the world where employees get designated US-flag-burning breaks.

Culture

Saudi Arabia's Islam culture is strictly observed by residents, and visitors to the country are expected to observe and respect religious customs in the same way. Most Westerners do their best to show due deference to a judiciary with a taste for capital punishment even the Bush boys would struggle to top. Beheadings, stonings and crucifixion are all approved methods. Amputations, the removal of teeth and floggings are prescribed for lesser crimes, such as drunkenness or immorality. The reality is that the only Westerners who don't consider the sharp end of Saudi culture to be barbaric in the extreme are those too scared to admit it.

Attractions

Riyadh has some impressive modern architecture, several striking works of modern art along the Corniche and arguably the world's largest airport. All of which are worth a look, providing you're male. If you're not, you better have a male in your party because you won't be allowed to drive.

Eating and Drinking

In a land where alcohol is forbidden, tea and coffee have become the number one stimulants. Expect to drink a lot of both and kiss the idea of getting any sleep goodbye.

Business or Business?

The question of what business you have going to Saudi Arabia needs to be taken quite literally, since without legitimate business you won't be let in. This does mean at least you don't have to worry about falling asleep on your connecting flight to Denver and winding up there by accident, but you probably won't want to think about trying to get in without having a very good reason for doing so.

To ease city congestion, Saudi Arabians were the first to hit on the 'Park and Ride' concept.

Sanaa

With the strict Islamic laws of Saudi, the crime levels of South America and the poverty of underdeveloped parts of Africa, Yemen has everything you could wish to avoid in a travel destination.

Country: Yemen	
Boredom Rating	★
Likelihood of Fatal Visit	★★★★
Essential Packing	Kaftan and qat leaves
Most Likely Cause of Death	Being a Westerner

History

Yemen has been a vital port since the first century AD. Its recent economic history has been linked closely to oil prices since commercial production facilities opened there in the mid-'90s. Needless to say, since then the economy has seen more crashes than an episode of *The Dukes of Hazzard*. A Persian kingdom that converted to Islam in the seventh century after the governor woke up with a bad hangover, it fell prey to the inevitable European attention in the 16th century and began the 20th century with an Ottoman-controlled northwest, a number of British-controlled protectorates, a host of insurgent sheikhs and a lot of overworked and very pissed-off mapmakers. The schisms imposed by competing usurpers led almost inevitably to permanent divisions, and in 1934 the Asir region became a part of Saudi Arabia and Yemen entered a period of depression and deprivation. By the dawn of the 1960s, the country as a whole had very few doctors, no public schools and was without a single paved road – making it a lot like modern-day Idaho.

Culture

Despite its efforts to establish itself as an oil boomtown, the real growth industry in Sanaa is kidnapping. While being abducted at gunpoint is

Men who pay their hairdressing bonus. Some of Sanaa's more recently grown on the back of their clients, without watching what of their clients.

never likely to be a fun experience no matter where you are, there is one big advantage to being taken hostage in Yemen – it's a lot cheaper than the same thing happening to you in Mexico. As befits Yemen's status as one of the world's poorest countries, ransoms come at knockdown prices here. A second-hand Mercedes, a month's supply of *qat* leaves, a cleaning job for a moronic cousin – all would be considered appropriate bounty for kidnappers in Sanaa. Unfortunately, on hearing such demands, your nearest and dearest may assume that they are being made the victims of a hidden-camera TV-show prank and start trying to spot the celebrity host when they should be reaching for their chequebooks. At this point you'll realise that however reasonable your captors' demands may have been, they're generally more than happy to get unreasonable in the event of non-payment.

Attractions

Tourists are usually safe in Yemen, provided they are sensible enough to stay away from areas frequented by tourists. This would rule out trips to Saana's most notable attractions, were it to have any.

Eating and Drinking

Most major socialising, like most political debate in the country, is done over extended *qat*-chewing sessions. This may go part of the way to explaining the political state the country is in, along with the sadly unremarkable range of cuisine on offer. Fortunately, chewing *qat* leaves also serves as an appetite suppressant.

Tehran

The first and only country in the world that saw going from Technicolor to monochrome as a step forwards.

Country: Iran	
Boredom Rating	★★★
Likelihood of Fatal Visit	★★★
Essential Packing	Everything black from your wardrobe
Most Likely Cause of Death	US air strike, by the time this book gets published

History

For years Iran was a bit-part player on the international stage with a premier who sounded like a character from *The Jungle Book*. But the course of its history changed forever in 1979: Islamic revolution swept the country and almost overnight the brutal, double-dealing monarchy became a brutal, double-dealing republic with an aversion to primary colours.

Left or right shoulder? How to wear your AK47 is a tough choice for Tehran's fashion-conscious youth.

Trifling allegations of sponsoring international terrorism aside, the Islamic presidency has remained relatively stable, despite managing to make enemies of both Iraq and the US and having to deal with the effects of an earthquake so catastrophic in scale that not even I'm prepared to make a cheap joke about it.

However, Tehran faces problems from an influx of cheap heroin from Afghanistan. The authorities claim that they are on top of the situation – no mean feat in a country where a day's hit costs less than a can of Coke and carries none of the stigma attached to such a Western product. By way of evidence, city health officials point to figures that suggest as many as 30 street-dwellers come off heroin every day. They claim that comparable figures for the number of dead bodies cleared from the streets each day are coincidental.

Culture

Iranian culture is largely Shi'ite. In contrast to many Western societies, government is happy to admit to that it would like to control every aspect of its people's everyday lives, including how they dress, what they eat and how many American flags they burn in a week. These codes are enforced by the *basij* – Islamic militia who act as a kind of extreme fashion police for a society where bad *hejab* – the flouting of Islamic dress codes – can mean a whole lot more than not getting invited over to Cassie's sleepover on Friday night.

However, a relaxation of such strict doctrines seems to be inevitable, at least as far as many young Iranians are concerned, and this is something that is increasingly being recognised by many of the city's cultural leaders. In recent years, this has led to several international designers being invited to give a more contemporary edge to the *chador*, the black shroud most Iranian women wear. Ralph Lauren enjoyed some success with his classic-with-a-twist update of the garment in charcoal grey. While many consumers responded positively to the cut and colour of the garment and to the addition of a mobile-phone

Michael Jackson is rarely recognised on his visits to Iran's capital.

pocket, they were less taken with the traditional stars-and-stripes detailing on the sleeve, and the item was outlawed by the *basij* having shifted only a few hundred units. Jean Paul Gaultier's take on the *chador* was notable for its Breton stripes, quirky hand-detailed stitching and ass-less chaps. Needless to say, the design only made it as far as the sample stage, which was submitted to the Ayatollah for approval, never to be seen again.

Attractions

Take a hike down the main street, Vali Asr – a 25-kilometre street that runs from the railway station to the northern foothills. Known as the Pahlavi until the 1979 Islamic revolution, it is the backbone of the city and you will see all life – or at least what passes for life – here. It is kept in relatively good condition by

the standard of Iranian roads, which might explain the traffic jams that start before dawn and end after dusk each day.

The Green Palace is in the Saadabad complex and is now a museum and coffee shop that has become an important meeting point for many of the older generations of Iraians who feel a certain nostalgia for their old monarchy. They admit that by and large the Shahs were all corrupt, brutal tyrants, but at least the outfits brought a bit of colour into their lives.

Outside the White Palace stands the statue of Reza Shah Pahlavi, father of the last Shah of Iran and said to be renowned in his day for his movie-star looks. The statue is modelled in bronze and currently ends just below the hips.

Eating and Drinking

For those on a tight budget, Friday is the day to head into town for free food – holy stew called *aash*, usually – from those mourning Shi'ite martyrs from 13 centuries ago. Try and avoid anniversaries of their demise, though, as these tend to get a little gory. Self-inflicted flagellation on a *Passion of the Christ* scale is pretty much expected from devotees in memory of whichever of the many martyrs they're remembering that day.

Festivals in Tehran

The Heart-Rending Departure of the Great Leader of the Islamic Republic of Iran is commemorated each June. Don't even think about taking to the streets unless you're great at keeping a straight face, as penalties for smiling during this period of mourning are particularly severe.

North America

EXPECT TO HEAR A NORTH AMERICAN SAY:
"We're Number One!"

MOST OBVIOUS LOW POINTS:
Artery-clogging food, George W. Bush,
no real history to speak of

SLIGHT COMPENSATIONS:
Large portions, Mickey Mouse, no real history to speak of

★★★★★	**GOD BLESS AMERICA**
★★★★	**YIPPIE-KI YAY!**
★★★	**MOR**
★★	**WHATEVER**
★	**AMERICAN PSYCHO**

Anchorage

Come to Anchorage for all the boredom of Nowheresville USA plus all the excitement of animal attacks that come with living on civilisation's fringes.

Boredom Rating	★★★★
Likelihood of Fatal Visit	★★★
Essential Packing	Snow shoes/tennis rackets
Most Likely Cause of Death	Brown bear/grizzly/local attack

History

Home to more than 40 percent of Alaska's population – which gives you at least some idea just how dreadful the rest of the state is – Anchorage began life as a cluster of tents used to shield the itinerant construction workers contracted to build the railroad. Neither the town's architecture nor its literacy rates have shown any significant improvement since then.

A town that's reaped the benefits of oil being discovered in the Cook Inlet in 1957, Anchorage is treated with a degree of contempt even by out-of-towners from the rest of the state, who see it as not really being a part of Alaska – an insult to the people of Anchorage that would be taken as a compliment everywhere else in the world.

Culture

Anchorage may just be every teenage boy's idea of heaven, with its weak American beer, numerous strip clubs and appalling climate giving a valid excuse for never going outside. But while the weather may have adversely affected the town's standing as a spring break getaway destination, it has helped to define the culture and people of the city.

This is serious frontiersman territory. Sled-dog racing, deer hunting and all the other associated sports based on animal cruelty are celebrated here, as is getting drunk as a skunk afterwards.

Attractions

If it's theatre you're after, then Mr. Whitekeys' Fly By Night Club has the one stage in town where the action doesn't purely revolve around women getting undressed in an uninterested way. In summertime, this is the venue for the long-running revue show *The Whale Fat Follies*, which can be quite amusing if you drink enough beforehand and are of the belief that quality entertainment begins and ends with fart jokes.

The Imaginarium's Earthquake Theatre may just be the most tasteless attraction in history, at least until the Twin Towers of Terror 9/11 Interactive experience gets approval for construction. Built as a tribute to those who suffered and died in the 9.2 Richter-scaled quake that hit the town in 1964, the attraction shuns the austere solemnity of its nearby rival, Earthquake Park, and goes for the jugular with a simulated quake of a feeble 4.6, about the equivalent of a household washing machine switching onto its spin cycle.

Eating and Drinking

If you're unlucky enough to find yourself in Anchorage for late summer, then head for the Ship Creek viewing platform east of the railroad depot. From here you can work up an appetite watching the king, poho and pink salmon swim desperately upstream. Round off your morning by heading downtown and ordering one of the plucky little buggers chargrilled with a nice green salad.

Atlantic City

Atlantic City is every bit as classy in real life as it's portrayed in the Louis Malle film that bears its name – in other words, it's full of dirty old men trying to cop off with desperate waitresses.

Country: New Jersey, USA

Boredom Rating	★★
Likelihood of Fatal Visit	★★★
Essential Packing	Marked deck
Most Likely Cause of Death	Pier collapsing

Bossing It

Atlantic City's favourite son is Bruce Springsteen, who made his name on the club circuit here in the early '70s. The Boss's albums are well worth checking out – not for his self-righteous janglings, but because the names of his tracks serve as an excellent guide on where to avoid on the East Coast in general.

History

Atlantic City was once considered the pleasure resort of choice for the East Coast rich and idle, but the rise of the low-cost air fares has seen it recognised for what it truly is – a tacky-sideshow built to stop conmen, no-hopers and other drifters from the West from falling into the ocean and instead put them to a job of work for which they are ideally suited. The state's decision to legalise casino gambling in 1978 represented a real desire both to encourage investment and to shift the town's population away from the prevalent lifestyle of drug addiction and unemployment, and was largely a success. The money-laundering business that follows the casino business wherever it gets the chance to ply its trade has given working mothers the opportunity to work 14-hour shifts round the clock while their kids play the slots in the lobby. And transforming the citizenry into alcoholic gambling addicts who have to hold down three such jobs just to keep up their loan-shark repayments has meant that the illegal economy is performing well enough to be listed on NASDAQ.

Culture

It's hard to escape from the blunt commercialism of the casino culture in Atlantic City, but since September 1921 the town has annually hosted the Miss America Pageant, taking the vulgarity factor of the area to such nausea-inducing levels that if you were anywhere but the USA you'd assume they were just being ironic.

Attractions

Atlantic City naturally attracts gamblers – and you've got to enjoy betting against the odds if you come to Atlantic City looking for a good time, as this is a place where you're never more than one-arm's length from a chance to lose your shirt. The house is obviously doing OK, because a lot of concrete has been poured recently, and it can't have all been motivated by the mob needing to get rid of bodies. The casinos are keen to improve the way they are perceived by holiday makers, and it's fair to say that Atlantic City is a great family destination – provided your family are all aged 21 or over.

New attractions include Smuggler's Cove, a themed development recalling the golden age of Prohibition and the place to go to see old mobsters getting dewy eyed about how much more fun Canadian whiskey runs were than breaking debtor's fingers. Le Jardin Palais is the most recent addition. Unfortunately, its attempts to bring up the area by giving itself a French name are sadly wasted on a populace that wouldn't recognise the language if it came in wearing a beret and a string of onions round its neck.

Atlantic City's annual sandcastle competition, where visitors often carve the destinations they'd sooner have gone on holiday to, if only they had enough money.

Self-proclaimed business genius Donald Trump is also well represented here. The Art Deco-themed Trump Marina and the Steel Pier form just two cornerstones in his Atlantic City empire, and in recent years he has found inspiration in the elaborately structured fretwork of the pier for creating his own bizarre hairstyle. The jewel in the Trump crown, however, is the Trump Taj Mahal, a gambler's Mecca fronted by nine limestone elephants. No expense was spared in the design and execution of these magnificent sculptures, though the application to have them carved from ivory was turned down as it was deemed to be in bad taste even by Atlantic City standards.

Eating and Drinking

Install yourself at a Blackjack table or allow yourself to be hypnotised by the spin of the roulette wheel and your time in Atlantic City will fly by, fortunately. Wall clocks are outlawed and the lighting carefully regulated. And with free 19-layer club sandwiches offered to high-rollers to encourage them to stay longer (and drop more) at the tables, and available very reasonably for everyone else, there's a good chance you won't make it out of the casino to sample the delights of Atlantic City's many dreadful restaurants. So maybe casino life does have something going for it after all.

Birmingham

Pardon me boys – is that the Chattanooga choo choo? Great, then I'm getting the hell outta here.

Boredom Rating	★★★★
Likelihood of Fatal Visit	★★
Essential Packing	"The South Will Rise Again" belt buckle
Most Likely Cause of Death	Hunting accident

History

With a motto guaranteed to strike fear into the heart of anyone crossing the state line and a flag that bears an uncanny resemblance to the cross of St. George, so beloved of English soccer hooligans, Alabama has been claimed briefly by the Spanish, English and French in its time, and then just as quickly disowned by swiftly retreating forces who denied ever having heard of it.

A key state in the American Civil War and contributor of 120,000 soldiers to the Confederate forces, its more recent history has been as a crucible for the civil rights struggles of the 1950s and '60s. The largest city in the state and county seat of Jefferson County, Birmingham was the site of a horrific church bombing by the Ku Klux Klan in 1963, which sadly helped disprove the theory that the pointy hats, long robes and sub-normal intelligence associated with Klan members prevented them from operating any equipment with more moving parts than a pitchfork.

Birmingham's police chief at the time, "Bull" Connor, took a depressingly predictable attitude to the inevitable protests and demonstrations of the period, using high-pressure hoses, cattle prods and Alsatians as his tools for healing the rifts in the community, and in doing so helped define a template for generations of Alabama men who were then just a twinkle in their father's/uncle's eye, usually on the same face.

Culture

While the election of five-term black mayor Richard Arrington has helped the city to put its history of racial conflict behind it, Birmingham still faces a number of challenges it looks barely up to handling. The state is culturally defined by its overwhelmingly protestant population and its constitution severely limits local government's ability to levy taxes. As a result of this reminder that the Lord helps those who help themselves, public services such as health, environment and transport are direly under funded, and therefore pretty useless. A 1956 amendment diverting cash garnered from petrol taxation into road building has led to the rise of the car in a state that rarely meets its targets on clean air. Meanwhile everyone's so busy paying medical bills for grandpa's emphysema that they can only afford crappy old pollution-mobiles. And such vehicles are the only mode of transport available to them since Birmingham's once-famous streetcar system became legendary – in the sense that no one quite knows if it ever actually existed or not. An $87 million grant has been approved – and may even have been already spent – but there's certainly no new mass-transit system to show for it if it has. Visitors are advised to rent a car and bring their own oxygen masks.

Attractions

Birmingham's claim to be the cultural and entertainment capital of Alabama is not surprisingly undisputed by Montgomery, Mobile or any other city in the state. The Birmingham Museum of Art is the Southeast's largest municipal art gallery and boasts the largest Wedgwood collection outside of England. A quick peek at this skip-load of prissy crockery and you'll appreciate why the English were so keen to get rid of it at the exorbitant price they charged.

Another of Birmingham's notable "attractions" is the Bessemer Hall of History's diverse collection of exhibits, which includes a mummy dating from the late 1970s and a typewriter that belonged to Adolf

Birmingham, Alabama – birthplace of the hardened artery.

Hitler. Expect all the educational value of a trip to Ripley's Believe it or Not, albeit with none of the entertainment value.

Eating and Drinking

The most powerful African American woman in the world today – with apologies to Oprah – hails from Birmingham, Alabama. And Condoleezza Rice speaks with great affection of the joys of Alabama cooking, which you can sample for yourself in one of the many home-style restaurants in Five Points South. That is if you're prepared to take the recommendation of a woman whose continued success in the Bush administration has led Michael Moore to consider calling his next book *Stupid White Men and One Woman Who Probably Sold Her Soul to Get Out of Birmingham*.

Medical History

The Alabama Museum of the Health Sciences features artefacts, specimens and instruments from as far back as the 16th century. Please note that this museum is open to the public from 9am–5.30pm only, as it serves as a state-of-the-art emergency room during the hours of darkness.

Charleston

Jesus is coming. Look busy.

Country: South Carolina, USA	
Boredom Rating	★★★★★
Likelihood of Fatal Visit	★
Essential Packing	Black Sabbath back catalogue
Most Likely Cause of Death	Plague of locusts

History

Charleston started its life as a port and plantation town handling the three commodities most beloved of the American south – cotton, rice and, of course, slaves. For 200 years it did brisk business and turned a healthy profit, but the Civil War put an end to that and a devastating earthquake in 1886 helped it down the road to becoming one of the US's poorest states.

Klan violence, frequent hurricanes and hungry mosquitoes have historically made it an extremely unpleasant place to live for all but the most conservative stay-at-homers, but this has not stopped it in recent years from attempting to sell itself as a tourist destination. And tumbling property prices – caused by the understandable ambitions of many residents to live anywhere but Charleston – have led in recent years to huge chunks of land around the town being converted into prime real-estate developments. These have proved immensely popular, considering the somewhat insalubrious surroundings – but then being one of America's haves is no fun unless you can flaunt the fact in front of the country's growing legions of have-nots.

Culture

Religion is big in South Carolina, and nowhere is this more in evidence than in Charleston and its surrounding neighbourhoods. Many of television's most powerful evangelists have been able to realise their dreams for a little piece of Heaven here on Earth. While Jim and Tammy Bakker's Christian theme park, Heritage USA, closed its gates for the last time in 1997, the area remains popular with televangelists looking to cash in on the trust their hapless followers place in them and take advantage of their tax-exempt status to turn a quick buck.

Attractions

Charleston is regularly up there in the Top Ten of most popular city destinations, though looking at the range of attractions available this is something of a mystery. Most of the city's finest houses are closed to the public, The Baruch Plantation's Slave Street is a depressing reminder of whose toil the city was built on, and Myrtle Beach is suitable only for anyone who likes being vomited on by teens on their spring break.

Outside of Charleston, the Rice Museum in Georgetown is open every day from 9.30am–4.30pm and is a great place for anyone looking to punish their children or subtly communicate to their partner that their relationship is going nowhere.

Eating and Drinking

Charleston's cuisine may not be mouth-watering, but it is certainly artery busting. Surf is generally indistinguishable from turf by the time it's been deep-fried, coated in cheese and dunked in sour cream, and is served up to a country music accompaniment that's almost as nauseatingly sweet as the desserts.

Dallas

The spiritual heart of the state that George W. Bush both cut his teeth and sealed his political reputation in. Need we say more?

Country: Texas, USA

Boredom Rating	★★★
Likelihood of Fatal Visit	★★★★
Essential Packing	A good lawyer or a watertight alibi
Most Likely Cause of Death	Lethal injection

History

It's impossible to talk about the city of Dallas without mentioning the two iconic men who were famously shot here before the very eyes of a shocked world. One was a charming yet highly amoral and famously oversexed man from an obscenely influential family. But while the assassination of JFK cast a shadow over the country and caused a nation to mourn, it was outdone in the ratings stakes 17 years later by the shooting of J.R. Ewing in the popular TV soap that bore the name of the city it was based in. Both of these events have played a part in making the state of Texas the most mythic in America, at least as far as Texans are concerned, despite the fact that audiences generally were unconvinced by the explanations given to them for either shooting.

Historically the site of many an epic battle between savage Native Americans and brave settlers armed only with Colt 45s and Winchester rifles, Dallas County was created in 1846. Central to its formation was John Neely Bryan, a Tennessee lawyer who sensed he might do good business in the area.

Nowadays, Dallas is renowned for its shopping, business and annual state fair, and is a haven of conspicuous consumption even by American standards. So, plenty for everyone lucky enough to find themselves above the poverty line – and precious little for anyone else.

It's the Law, Buddy

Travellers are reminded that the following are illegal in the state of Texas:

Gambling (Class-C misdemeanour punishable by a fine of up to $500)

Possession of six or more sex toys (as this qualifies you as a wholesaler of said items)

Same-sex sex (punishable by a fine of up to $500)

Draining oil onto the ground during oil changes

Sodomy (same-sex or heterosexual)

On a more positive note, bestiality – unlike same-sex sex – is not considered "deviate" under Texas law.

Culture

When they're not too busy trying to kill each other, Texans are among the friendliest people on the planet and small talk is considered mandatory wherever you go in the city. Chatting with Texans, you'll soon find they've got hearts as big as their ten-gallon hats and mouths and opinions to match. Unfortunately, this may not leave you with a huge amount of space to express your own thoughts. However, storytelling is a long-held tradition in Texas, and coupled with its strongly held fundamental Christian beliefs, helps to make Texans among the most entertaining speakers you'll ever come across – as anyone who's seen honorary Texan George W. Bush attempt to explain fiscal policy can testify to. The Texas Education Department has a

Hank Fryden, winner of Dallas 'Slimmer of the Year' for five consecutive years since 2001

tendency to view most textbooks on "questionable" subjects such as evolution, quantum mechanics and (non-local) geography as fuel for the barbecue, so you can hardly blame them for having a limited view of the world. Get a Texan onto a subject of interest such black holes, say, or the origin of dinosaurs and sit back knowing you're in for an interesting tale.

Attractions

The Lone Star state has long cherished its reputation for dealing out frontier justice, and there's something here for everyone with an interest in death, segregation and state-sponsored murder who can't be bothered to make the trip to Saudi Arabia. Take a whistle-stop tour of the penal institution's capital-punishment facilities, whose prodigious output have earned them a place in the *Guinness Book of World Records* for executing more prisoners than any other state, and the surrounding countryside, where some of the grisliest lynchings in America's troubled past took place. Or stroll along Dealey Plaza to the Conspiracy Museum, where you can learn all about the CIA's (alleged) involvement in the assassination of America's most popular president of modern times.

The state's legal department remains unapologetic about its record and maintains that anyone who finds themselves on the wrong side of the law in a capital-crime case in Dallas is guaranteed a fair trial by a jury of their peers, followed very quickly by a first-class execution. They also point to the fact that their penal institutions have always been quick to move with the times, being the first state to adopt both the electric chair and the lethal injection, though it took a few very messy executions for the authorities to realise they didn't actually need to use both simultaneously.

Eating and Drinking

A number of exciting restaurants have opened in downtown Dallas in recent years, ranging from those with a pan-Pacific menu to a couple of authentic French-styled bistros and the state's first Michelin-starred eatery. Sadly, these have all closed down due to lack of business. If you're after food in Dallas you can choose between two major food types – stuff that's barbecued and potato salad. Some of Dallas' more adventurous diners have even been known to combine the two.

The birthplace of Motown and the motorcar, two things that helped define the United States but which now seem to be in terminal decline.

Boredom Rating	★★★★
Likelihood of Fatal Visit	★★
Essential Packing	Furry dice
Most Likely Cause of Death	Exhaust fumes

History

Boasting the finest array of boarded-up buildings in the developed world and evocative in odour of Sylvia Plath's last few moments on earth, Detroit is a city with a past as colourful as its present is a sickly shade of grey. Named after the nearby convergence of Lake St. Clair with Lake Erie, the city's 200 years of slow, steady growth got a jolt in the arm with the arrival of Henry Ford. The Ford Motor Company revolutionised the automobile industry – assembly-line construction enabled the workforce to work faster and smarter, at least for the couple of years before the formation of the first auto workers' union led to them working slower and worse. And the innovations of the company spread out into the city that surrounded the plant – in 1909, Detroit became the first city in America to have a paved concrete road. In 1915, it became the first to install a traffic light. And later that same year, it became the first city to recognise the raising of the middle finger as censure for a fellow road-user's driving inabilities. Ted Dixley, the man credited with inventing the gesture, was also a keen linguist, who was forever on the lookout for ways to expand and invigorate the English language. His oft-quoted phrase "The light was red you c***-****ing mother******!" is one used and enjoyed by the people of the city to this day.

Culture

Detroit's proximity to Canada made it an important stop for African American slaves looking to escape the yoke of slavery before Abolition, and this is reflected in the city's rich cultural life. The town's importance as a jazz and blues Mecca was cemented by the arrival of Mississippi's finest blues man, John Lee Hooker, in the 1940s. While his attempt to create a new upbeat fusion sound on his little-heard Detroit album *I Love My Life and Everybody Loves Me* was neither a critical nor a commercial success, Hooker's return to a more traditional blues sound on *Please Lord, End it Now* was, and the market for up-tempo pop was soon to be filled by the emergence of Motown, the first major-league African American label. Their high profile throughout the '50s and '60s was based on innovative

The Power of Three

The three heavyweights of the American motor industry – Ford, GM and Chrysler – have all responded to the challenge of high-quality, low-cost imports from Japan by spending massive amounts on research and development in order to give drivers exactly what they want. Their key findings show that whilst most consumers are looking for competitively priced, easy-to-park saloons with low CO_2 emissions, one key demograph – mothers with pre-teen children – were only interested in turbo-charged, diesel, four-wheel drive SUVs with tinted windows, in-car entertainment systems and ear-splitting horns "to do the school run in." Their response to this piece of research is to create ever bigger SUVs, because it's "more fun".

production, solid song-writing and the creation of an incredible roster of artists, including Marvin Gaye, the Four Tops and Michael Jackson. In the '70s and '80s, the company sought to build on their success by signing Kiki Dee, The Dazz Band and Bruce Willis. Perhaps not surprisingly, the company was sold to Polygram in 1993, and its former headquarters is now just one of the many empty buildings in Detroit with cardboard double-glazing.

Attractions

As you might expect, Motor City is designed first and foremost for drivers. Pedestrians actually come fourth in order of priority, after trucks and helicopters, despite the fact that no one has seen a whirlybird since the police called in the National Guard during the riots of '67. So it's worth driving to Detroit's two big tourist draws, the Henry Ford Museum and Kellogg's Cereal City USA, particularly since the low-interest value of either of these so-called attractions means that getting a parking space is rarely a problem.

The Detroit Zoo was once famous for its refusal to cage animals, opting instead for a network of moats, thick undergrowth and natural features to keep the animals from eating between meals. This may have seemed like a good idea during the city's golden age, but its faded fortunes now makes the combination of dangerously lax safety measures and increasingly hungry animals a chilling prospect for anyone hoping to return home with all of their children.

Eating and Drinking

There are still a couple of restaurants operating in Detroit. Diners are usually asked to pay in advance. Those traveling on a budget may be interested in the all-the-burnt-toasted-cereal-you-can-eat offer available to anyone taking the Kellogg's tour.

To eliminate confusion for those shopping whilst drunk: BEER is on the LEFT. WINE is on the RIGHT.

Edmonton

Anyone who says Canada is a duller, colder, more expensive version of the USA doesn't know what they're talking about ... or is talking about Edmonton.

Country: Alberta, Canada

Boredom Rating	★★★★
Likelihood of Fatal Visit	★
Essential Packing	Checked shirt
Most Likely Cause of Death	Faulty elevator

History

Edmonton is a former Albertan backwater best known historically for the trial of Elisabeth Sawyer, a woman accused of bewitching the children and cattle of her neighbours so that they would buy her brooms. Her somewhat aggressive approach to direct marketing got her into a kangaroo court where her lawyer's advice to "cop a plea" was to go down in legal history as the worst decision ever made. Elisabeth Sawyer's confession earnt her a trip to the gallows in 1621, and the people of Edmonton have been struggling to find an entertainment to match up to public hanging ever since, though the continuing popularity of ice hockey has gone someway to satisfying their bloodlust.

Culture

For many people, Canada is a slightly forlorn expanse of frozen rock sporadically peppered with people who both resent and envy their American neighbours to the south. But this is only seven-eighths of the story. Most Canadians base their opinions of Americans on the draft-dodgers within their own communities and so see them all as weed-smoking layabouts. In return, the USA is suspicious of any country that questions the authority of Rupert Murdoch's "fair and balanced" Fox News, especially when 25 percent of its population is French speaking.

Attractions

Most of Alberta is keen to emphasise the outdoors, but Edmonton, which boasts several of the world's largest malls, refuses to let mountainous landscapes, Arctic temperatures or dangerous wildlife stop anyone taking out extortionate store credit for items they don't need. The visitor will be able to get everything here except mobile phone coverage.

Eating and Drinking

Contrary to uninformed popular opinion, Canadians don't only eat doughnuts and maple syrup. But you should unless you want your gut to still be digesting curried moose-head by the time you get home.

Gold Rush Boomtown

A promise of gold and knock-down property prices in 1870 led to the town's expansion, peaking during the Klondike Gold Rush of 1897, at which point the town of Edmonton was finally recognised as being a crappy one-horse town in the back end of nowhere. Still, there was nowhere else to buy supplies and it was declared the provincial capital in 1905, narrowly beating a shack next to a frozen lake on the outskirts of Banff.

Anyone still uncertain about whether or not socialism is still a viable cure for the planet's woes has probably never tried ordering room service in Havana.

Boredom Rating	★★★
Likelihood of Fatal Visit	★★
Essential Packing	Cigar cutters
Most Likely Cause of Death	Coma induced by televised Castro speech

History

A mere 105 miles southwest of Key West, Florida, Cuba has made a career of contradicting the USA. And while the rest of the planet may secretly delight in the fact that the world's sole superpower has never shown itself capable of policing the miscreant on its own front doorstep, it's hard to see how this stance has benefited the common population of the island that Che and Cas so firmly believed in advancing the cause of.

Cuba was the number-one Spanish New World colony for all but a brief year from 1762, when the island was seized by the British Navy before being quickly traded back in exchange for Florida, three cases of rum and a particularly accommodating donkey called Paco.

The island's reputation as a party destination was cemented during Prohibition in the 1920s when Havana was flooded with the great and good of the USA looking to forget the troubles of the booze-free society they were imposing on everyone back home. This was usually done with the help of a few beers and a *mojito* or seven. Revolution at the dawn of the 1960s brought an ideologically driven socialist government to power and revived calls stateside for the invasion that had seemed imminent since

Jefferson had been getting his jollies with White House day staff. Efforts by the CIA to destabilise the new regime proved ineffective, and one botched invasion by genetically engineered amphibious pigs later, Uncle Sam was once again able to earn himself the title not only of world's biggest bully but also of history's crappiest superpower. The promise of reprisals from Soviet missiles on Cuban turf was deemed serious enough to distract JFK from his busy social diary for a couple of weeks at least, but while overt armed hostilities between the two nations have remained low key and sporadic, economic sanctions have helped keep Cuba's development frozen sometime in the mid-20th century.

Culture

Wherever you go in Havana there's an air of faded opulence. Many of the once-grand buildings are notable for their peeling paint, crumbling plasterwork and missing walls. Many others are in more serious need of repair, however. Cubans have done the best

they can to maintain Havana's stately architectural legacy with whatever is at hand. As all that is usually at hand is the lump of masonry that narrowly missed landing on them, the best they can generally manage is to arrange said brickwork in neat little piles by the side of the potholed mess of a road.

Despite high unemployment, inadequate public health facilities and TV schedules that alternate government propaganda with news bulletins, weather forecasts and chat shows all hosted by the country's premier, Cuban culture is underlined by a strong sense of optimism. Whether this highlights the essential indomitability of the human spirit or is merely the result of viral bacteria in the untreated water supply, Cubans are grateful people. And they

insist that you be the same while visiting. Taxi drivers, boatmen and airline pilots will expect a tip before you set off and a round of applause for delivering you to your destination still breathing.

Attractions

Choose between the rampant decay of the city centre and the gentle degradation of the old town. The former will appeal if you're in the market for a sexually transmitted infection from one of the city's under-age prostitutes, while in the latter you may catch one of the daily sideshows that accompanies the collapse of a tenement-housing development.

Eating and Drinking

Cuba's reputation as a party town may have something to do with the fact that most Cubans do their drinking, along with all their other activities, on an empty stomach.

Government vehicles in Cuba are legally required to pick up hitchhikers if they have the space. However, this rarely happens in Havana, as government officials are the best-fed people in Cuba and have enough trouble squeezing themselves and their entourages into their air-conditioned limos.

Los Angeles

The City of Angels has been peddling the world its dreams for more than a century, but it's a nightmare for anyone who lives there.

Country: California, USA

Boredom Rating	★
Likelihood of Fatal Visit	★★★★
Essential Packing	Vice (for maintaining a grip on reality)
Most Likely Cause of Death	Smog asphyxiation

History

The Town of Our Lady the Queen of the Angels of the Porciúncula River was formed in 1781, although it was not until 1786 that elections were held and Jose Vanega became the first mayor. His first executive order was to horsewhip the working committee who'd come up with such a dumb name for the town.

The shortened moniker may seem something of a bad joke for anyone forced to live in such a hellhole, but it did at least stop the population from rioting, which is generally seen as a glowing achievement for any elected officer in this city.

Culture

The sprawl of low-rise Americana we now know as LA is actually the 44 independent cities that make up LA County. Many visitors express concern that parts of the city are dangerous and worry about accidentally taking a wrong turn into a gang-controlled area. Such worrying is generally uncalled for, since it doesn't matter what turn you take you'll be in the wrong part of town – it's all gang controlled.

Happily race is no longer an issue. Los Angeles had set the national benchmark for race rioting in the past, but while the 1992 riots were set off in part by a racially targeted attack by the most brutal armed gang in the hood – or the LAPD, as they're generally known – once the citizens got involved it became a

The recent dodgy exhaust pipe and faulty catalytic converter crackdown resulted in 82 percent of the cars in LA being repossessed.

truly multicultural affair, with men of all colours and creeds united in their love of looting high-priced electrical goods.

Los Angeles may not be a melting pot – in truth it's more of a compartmentalised Tupperware container struggling to keep its contents from spilling over into other's sections – but in the last few years the gangs have cleaned up their act and inter-gang hostilities are now infrequent. So you can wear whatever colours you feel like, safe in the knowledge that the gangs all now have their Kel-Tec P11 pistols aimed not at each other, but squarely at you – until you produce your wallet.

Carbon footprint? What carbon footprint? You can't get away from it all in a gas guzzling hire car in a country where the right to produce smog is written into the constitution.

Ordering Food in La La Land

Once your waiter has introduced himself, asked if you would like to see the specials menu and pitched his screenplay idea, you may order. LA is the spiritual centre of the politically correct universe, so you should try to avoid using potentially inflammatory language. Abstain from using words like "black" (offensive to African Americans), "red" (offensive to Native Americans), "breast", "thighs", "rack", "buns", "rump", "melon", "meat" and "spit-roast" (offensive to women's groups), "fruit", "pink" and "faggot" (offensive to homosexuals) and any use of French terms or language at all.

Attractions

Despite the city's shallow image, there is some remarkable and deeply soul-stirring art to be found in LA, namely in the Getty Museum. A short drive into the Santa Monica mountains and set in 110 acres of lush countryside, it houses paintings, photography and installation works. They are easily viewed as local visitors will be spending their time checking out each other and themselves in the many reflective surfaces.

There is, of course, one place you can go if you are looking for culture you can share with an appreciative audience. LAX is, not surprisingly, one of the best served airports in the world, and a domestic flight to any destination will take you somewhere with more cultural depth than LA.

Eating and Drinking

Downtown LA boasts some of the finest restaurants on the West Coast, though many may require you to book well in advance – speculative bookings, such as for your unborn child's 21st birthday celebrations, are not unheard of. Most restaurants offer free parking, but try to avoid driving through the rougher parts of South Central after nightfall, as it tends to become gridlocked with documentary film crew vans.

Mitchell

The former frontier lands of Crazy Horse and Sitting Bull have been usurped by the demands of the paleface for Running Water (in every room) and Rolling Fairway (strictly members only).

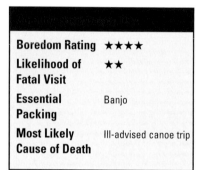

Boredom Rating	★★★★
Likelihood of Fatal Visit	★★
Essential Packing	Banjo
Most Likely Cause of Death	Ill-advised canoe trip

History

The people of the USA – military personnel aside – may be the least travelled people on the planet, with only 18 percent of the adult population even owning a passport. But they have the excuse, at least, of being the product of unadventurous ancestors, who, having made it as far as they had, wasted no time in building themselves faux-European houses that were identical to the ones they had left behind. They then stirred from the safety of these homes only to repel the odd tomahawk attack.

By the turn of the 19th century, most Americans' knowledge of what made up the frontier territories was as shaky as their concept of Native American rights. So when Lewis and Clark set off up the Missouri river in a second-hand keelboat, they had no idea what would confront them. What they found, in South Dakota at least, was coyotes, prairie dogs and pronghorns – runty, goat-like antelopes that look suspiciously like the product of an unholy union between a coyote and a prairie dog.

Lewis and Clark's disappointing start to their great adventure then threatened to be cut short in the first act when the discoverers were discovered themselves by a tribe of less-than-welcoming Teton Sioux. With all the certainty of the great statesmen that would follow them, they assured the gathered elders that they were on a mission of peace, and after greasing palms with bottles of whisky they were allowed to take their swivel-cannon-armed boat and regiment of musket-bearing troops further upriver on their journey of peaceful discovery.

Culture

With more than 60,000 American Indian residents in the state today, South Dakota's culture is not surprisingly dominated by its Wild West past, and the legend of the Sioux struggles has pricked many a modern liberal conscience.

Kevin Costner risked his (then) unblemished reputation and a fair sum of his own dollars on bringing the story of the Sioux's eviction and exploitation to the big screen in *Dances With Wolves*. His remarkable success at the Oscars and at the box office brought the plight of the native peoples of America sharply into focus for a contemporary audience, and allowed Costner the freedom to develop his plans for an 838-acre recreation resort in the Black Hills of South Dakota, to the immense chagrin of the people whose case he had supposedly pleaded.

Mount Rushmore

If the lack of tourist traps in Mitchell leaves you feeling restless, jump on Interstate 90 and head out to Black Hills National Forest for a look at Mount Rushmore. In the faces of Washington, Jefferson, Lincoln and Roosevelt you can see an echo of America's current leader. Like Bush, they too seem to spend most of their time staring blankly out into the middle distance as if confused by what they're reading on their giant, though unseen, auto cues.

The remoteness of Mitchell's surroundings and its lack of passing travellers make it the perfect place for disposing of unwanted spouses.

Attractions

If you're looking for something to do to pass the time, you probably won't want to start your search in Mitchell, a town as devoid of things to do as a timeshare salesman on death row. The Corn Palace on Main Street has claimed it is the world's largest birdfeeder, a claim to fame that few people would deny them the right to given its limited ambition. Admission, not surprisingly, is free.

Eating and Drinking

Most of the town's restaurants – and indeed most of the whole town – are to be found on Main Street. The Depot Grill and Pub has proved to be a big hit with the hunting community since it opened in 1990. It offers precisely the atmosphere and level of comfort you would find in a railroad passenger and freight depot from 1900, as well as most of the original plumbing.

New York City

Some day maybe a real rain will come and wash all the scum off the streets. At which point maybe it might be nice to go to New York. But until that happens, fuggeddaboudid.

Country: New York, USA	
Boredom Rating	★
Likelihood of Fatal Visit	★★
Essential Packing	Wristwatch with second hand set to New York minute
Most Likely Cause of Death	Heart attack

History

Fumbling around in search of the Northwest Passage in 1609, Henry Hudson came upon Manhattan and its surrounding lands and declared that it was "as beautiful a land as one can hope to tread upon". Four hundred years and a whole lot of treading later, NYC has survived draft riots during the Civil War, the threat of being named New Amsterdam and the phallic fixation of successive generations of architects. Not to mention the most horrendous terrorist attack to be witnessed in modern times. None of which should distract the modern traveller from avoiding it at all costs. Don't be lured by the promise of low-price air fares, great shopping, the fantastic architecture and the possibility of running into cool celebrities. New York winters have been killing people since the Pilgrim Fathers first pitched camp, but they are still preferable to summers in this sweatbox of a city, making it a place with a climate that's tolerable for about two weeks of the year, one in April and one in October.

Culture

The American Film Industry may have chosen to locate itself on the West Coast, but NYC is undoubtedly the most filmed city in movie history. Oliver Stone, Ridley Scott, Spike Lee, Woody Allen, Martin Scorcese and John Schlesinger are among a host of directors to have produced remarkable works that could probably be set nowhere else in the world, and which have helped to enhance the Big Apple's iconic status in the eyes of the world. All of which gives you a first-class reason for staying home and renting a bunch of DVDs rather than heading to New York in the mistaken belief that the bricks and mortar will actually match up to the celluloid fantasy.

Post 9/11, tourism is down in the city and even the promise of another pointless piece of public art in Central Park by Christo has failed to reverse this trend. However, this hasn't stopped New Yorkers from going about their daily business with the same blend of aggression and intolerance as ever, and despite the fact that cabbies the world over have modelled their can't-do attitude on depictions of their Manhattan counterparts, there really is still no topping the original and best when it comes to an appallingly low level of customer service served up with a side of inventive profanity.

Attractions

No visit to New York City is complete without a trip to the Empire State Building. This at least must be the current advice to all travellers to the city, as whatever time of day or night you might choose to head there you'll be met with the kind of queues you

Manhattan Manners

Like all New Yorkers, chefs and waiters have been affected by years of personal-space deprivation and can be a little "in your face". Order promptly, make no special requests, eat whatever is brought to you and tip at least 15 percent and you may just make it out of your eatery without being publicly humiliated or assaulted.

If you can't make it to Whistler or Vermont, never mind – there is often enough snow in wintertime New York for the hardened *langlauf* cross-country ski enthusiast.

thought died out with the breadlines in Russia. Head to the observation level on the 102nd floor for a cheek-to-cheek romantic tryst with your loved one and whoever happens to be forced up against you in the lift. If your craving for tall buildings is still not sated, head for the Statue of Liberty. The 354 steps to the top should have you pining for your hotel, and with similar queues of people you'll know how it feels to be one of the huddled masses yearning to breath free in no time.

Central Park used to be a great place to unwind, score some angel dust or get mugged, but the introduction of zero-tolerance policing means that loitering laws are now strictly enforced. In any case the air is a lot less fresh since every smoker in the city started heading there on their lunch break.

Eating and Drinking

New York has some fantastic restaurants, lively delis and atmospheric coffee bars. However, contrary to what you may have seen on TV, spacious leather sofas are hard to come by. In fact, most New Yorkers would have trouble finding space for any kind of sofa in their cell-size "studio" apartments. Expect to be eating in close proximity to your fellow diners and be prepared to synchronise your elbow movements with theirs.

Orlando

Contrary to popular belief, Orlando does have some history. Some of the motel pillows are nearly 40 years old.

Boredom Rating	n/a: Being bored has been officially outlawed in Florida – anyone caught in this state (in this state) is subject to a heavy fine.
Likelihood of Fatal Visit	★
Essential Packing	Ruby-red slippers
Most Likely Cause of Death	Saccharine poisoning

History

An important outpost during the Seminole Wars of the early part of the 19th century, the small community of Jernigan registered for a name change in 1857. It chose to take the name of an American Army Sentinel who had famously got on the wrong end of an arrow. Other than that, little evidence remains of the city's small-town roots – in 1875 its population numbered a mere 85, which would register only as a small queue for the water fountain in today's Orlando.

But whatever happened in the past is of little interest to the people and businesses of the city today, who are more concerned with how much of your hard-earned cash you're planning on parting with in the present and immediate future. History is tolerated only as long as it can be represented with animatronics and, preferably, feature dinosaurs.

Culture

There's no escaping the mouse. All roads lead to him. His presence looms over everything and signs for the Magic Kingdom hang over every interstate and slip road like crucified slaves on the Appian Way. Culturally, if you're not into Walt Disney's nightmare made reality – or the various bargain-basement versions of it that are found skulking around the fringes of Orlando like unwanted dogs the day after Christmas – then you should probably be asking yourself what you were thinking when you booked your trip in the first place.

Florida has some of the largest multiplex cinemas in the world showing all the latest Hollywood releases, ranging from dumb teen comedies to moronic action flicks. So, whatever your preference, there's bound to be something to suit you – providing you have the tastes of a Neanderthal. Plans are also underway for Orlando's first bookshop, due to open in the spring of 2009 (subject to planning approval).

Attractions

Excitement is just around every corner, particularly now that Florida has become officially recognised as the most dangerous state in the USA in which to be a pedestrian. Having a car is therefore essential as it gives the city's criminal fraternity the option to take something that isn't your life. Should you manage to make it to one of Orlando's many amusement parks without being robbed, you can rest assured that you will spend the rest of the day being ripped off on the price of hot dogs and sodas.

While the rides are constantly being changed within Orlando's many theme parks to keep up with an ever-demanding public, many popular ones have become institutions in their own right. And an institution is precisely where you'll feel like checking into once you've completed a circuit of It's a Small World.

Eating and Drinking

Whatever you eat in Orlando, you can guarantee that it will perfectly capture the flavour of the town – that is, it will be overpriced, artificial and of no intrinsic value whatsoever.

The city of Orlando boasts the largest population of otherwise unemployable actors of any state in the USA, with the exception of Washington, D.C.

Home of the Hurricane

Florida has been hit by so many hurricanes in its short history that they've run out of girl's names for them and have had to resort to using boy's!

Rhyolite

A once-thriving community that's now a virtual ghost town. And with very good reason too.

Country: Nevada, USA

Boredom Rating	★★★★
Likelihood of Fatal Visit	★★
Essential Packing	Geiger counter
Most Likely Cause of Death	Unexploded thermo-nuclear device

The Superior log cabin shown here is available to rent from June through August, once Hank finishes over-wintering his hog, Jezebel.

History

A pretty desert town from a distance, Rhyolite, like so many parts of America, is truly terrifying up close. Founded in 1900 to serve as a railway centre for the Bullfrog Mining Community, it boasted a population of 10,000. But when the price of frogs, toads, newts and related amphibians was sent tumbling by the rise of South American imports, the mine and three railroads that served it went out of business. Today, the population is officially nil, although it is certainly popular with the coyotes. Which goes to show that whatever else we might learn from watching cartoons, they got it right when they portrayed the coyote as a stupid creature with a short life expectancy. For Rhyolite is just a short gust of wind beyond the buffer zone surrounding the Nevada Test Site, a mere 30 miles or so from its epicentre.

Culture

As you might expect from somewhere this close to Death Valley, there's a sense on the streets of Rhyolite that the Grim Reaper has taken up permanent residence here – or if not, then he must regularly rent a cottage for the weekend. Spend five minutes on Main Street and you'll be expecting the Mystery Machine to pull up. According to US defence sources, any permanent residents located outside the buffer zone are at no risk from contamination – in fact, the town of Beatty lies several miles east of Rhyolite and with its population of 1,500 is a relative metropolis for the region.

However, the Nevada Test Site has the smallest budget of any nuclear weapons facility in the USA, despite the fact that it uses the same advanced technology for disposing of its radioactive waste as other centres – which consists of digging a big hole and burying it. The administrators of the nation's primary commercial site for clowning about with nuclear explosives in the name of military science maintain that they follow stringent safety procedures at all times and have certainly never fallen foul of any full-scale environmental impact studies conducted at the dump in Beatty. This would probably be because no such full-scale environmental impact studies have ever been carried out.

A weekend's drinking in Rhyolite can often be combined with a DIY project – the two heady pursuits of most local residents.

Attractions

Rhyolite's major attraction – after the pondful of fish with three eyes – is the Bottle House. Built in 1906 from 50,000 beer bottles, it stands as a monument to what the miners spent their time doing when they weren't mining. It is remarkable by Nevada's construction standards in that it was not only completed ahead of schedule, it was actually completed before anyone had even had time to come up with one.

Eating and Drinking

There are no restaurants in Rhyolite, so there's nothing to eat – unless you're into raw tumbleweed, that is. And you probably shouldn't drink the water either.

Miss Trailer Park USA

Without doubt, the biggest local event of the year is the Miss Beatty Pageant, held in September. Contestants from the "big town", as Beatty is known, compete with itinerant residents of the area's many ill-placed trailer parks. With such a small, tight-knit community, the evidence of an unhealthily small gene pool is all too apparent in the too-close eyes and oversized foreheads of the contestants, and it is an unusual year when the winner is not related to her predecessor by either blood or marriage – which often amounts to the same thing.

Washington, D.C.

Getting to Washington, D.C., couldn't be easier as it's served by three major airports: Washington Dulles International, Ronald Reagan Washington National and one other I forget.

Boredom Rating	★★★★
Likelihood of Fatal Visit	★★
Essential Packing	Wiretap-tracing equipment
Most Likely Cause of Death	Asking too many questions

History

The capital city and administrative district of the USA, Washington, D.C., accommodates the official residence of the President and First Lady, the centres of all three branches of the US Federal Government, the headquarters of the majority of federal agency headquarters, the central office of the International Monetary Fund and 54 Starbucks, none of which has had a seat vacant since 1991. An estimated 73 percent of the local work force are engaged directly in government or judicial employment with a further 18 percent working in essential associated industries such as information technology, canvassing and three-hour dry cleaning.

Culture

Whatever your feelings may be about US governments past or present, it's fair to say that the atmosphere of the city reflects the colourful events going on in the corridors of power. A frequent winner of the hotly contested title of Murder Capital USA, the city is as bedevilled by poverty and allegations of racial discrimination as Congress is by allegations of filibustering and sexual harassment. With a former

The statue of former president Abraham Lincoln. Lincoln did many famous things in his time, though most will remember him for his guest-starring appearance in *Bill & Ted's Big Adventure*.

Washington just doesn't know how to build small – everything is on an epic scale. Shown here, the Greek Revival crazy golf kiosk.

mayor who suffered from not only being christened with a girl's name, but also being caught on videotape smoking crack, there's every chance that Washington's most remarkable cultural distinction is that everyday conversation is now regarded as being of such potential value that you are likely to be recorded wherever you are.

Attractions

If pompous-looking buildings, overblown avenues and libraries you need a golf cart to get around in aren't your thing, then you should probably have stayed away from Washington altogether. However, a hatred of all things official goes down very well at the numerous demonstrations and barmy splinter-movement meetings that take place in the city. January brings the Martin Luther King, Jr. day, when orators take turns to recite King's seminal "I have a dream" speech karaoke style, proving that the maxim "they don't write them like that anymore" applies to speech writing as much as to popular music.

Eating and Drinking

As befits its status, Washington, D.C., has a number of restaurants that serve excellent food. Which is more than can be said for the service on offer once you get there. Expect your order to be incorrect and to arrive with all the haste of a constitutional amendment not linked to the War on Terror getting onto the statute book.

Birth of a Nation

Washington, D.C., was established as the seat of government in 1790 as a natural midpoint between north and south. The fact that the newly created meeting place was also conveniently located just over the river from the home of the new president – after whom the district was also named – was, of course, purely coincidental.

LET'S NOT GO TO...

South America

EXPECT TO HEAR A SOUTH AMERICAN SAY:
"Tequila!"

MOST OBVIOUS LOW POINTS:
Kidnappings, poor transport network,
poor record on human rights

SLIGHT COMPENSATIONS:
Carnivals, cheap accommodation, improving record on
human rights – as if it could have got any worse

OVERALL RATING: ★★★

★★★★★	**OLÉ!**
★★★★	**THE (BRAZIL) NUTS**
★★★	**COKE AND A SMILE**
★★	**ARGIE-BARGIE**
★	**HASTA LA VISTA, BABY**

Buenos Aires

Argentina's recent history reads all too much like the life of Diego Maradona, the nation's footballing legend. Blessed with abundant natural resources, it has spent the last few years looking for new ways to piss them away.

Country: Argentina

Boredom Rating	★
Likelihood of Fatal Visit	★★★
Essential Packing	I luv Islas Malvinas t-shirt
Most Likely Cause of Death	Plummeting ruined businessman

History

Like many South American states, Argentina has gone through military coups like Naomi Campbell goes though personal assistants. The most famous of these saw Juan Perón and his pushy wife Eva getting kicked out of office in 1955, resulting in great deal of suffering and misery. But leaving an evening at the theatre watching *Evita* to one side for the moment, the military junta's 30-year stewardship of the country also led to internal strife, the abduction of political dissidents and industrial action on a scale that you'd expect from a nation state of air traffic controllers. The Dirty War of the late '70s resulted in the disappearance of more than 20,000 Argentine citizens and, while it did improve the unemployment figures for a brief time, it left many people with a deep mistrust of the administration.

Things took a turn for the worse in 1979. In a move that remains popular with dictators and "democratically elected" presidents alike, General Leopold Galtieri attacked a defenceless patch of land in order to distract the electorate from the dreadful mismanagement of domestic affairs. Unfortunately, he picked the wrong bit of land. No oilfields have yet been discovered on or around the Falkland Islands and in fact the only natural resource it's abundant in is sheep s**t. He also picked the wrong British Prime Minister to take on: Margaret Thatcher in her prime was fearsome enough to put the willies up even the most hardened Argentine torturer. While she generally prefers her relations with South American dictators to be cordial in the extreme, she was more than happy to commit British troops to an outpost that was pointless even by the standards of the British Empire.

You can't beat those lusty Latins when it comes to the passionate intensity of the Tango.

Culture

Despite a background of economic chaos and the largest outstanding VISA bill in history, Buenos Aires has taken on the challenges of the 21st century with a fresh face – a face it changes every few weeks, it would seem, given the average length of office for presidents in Buenos Aires. But this lack of stability may be what fires that most obvious embodiment of Argentine culture, the Tango. Instability certainly seems to be central to the dance as it's performed by the average visiting European.

While tedious garden designers exhort us to make outdoor rooms of gardens, in Buenos Aires they have swung the other way and taken the great outdoors inside.

The music of the Tango can be heard wherever you go on the needlessly broad avenues of Buenos Aires, and the people of the city love nothing more than to cast their work and cares aside for a moment and dance spontaneously to its tantalising rhythms. This means that you're liable to encounter some very friendly bus conductors, not to mention some extremely dangerous directing of traffic in the Plaza de la Republica.

Attractions

While Spanish is the predominant language of the country, Buenos Aires is a diverse and all-embracing city. Wander the bohemian streets of the San Telmo *barrio* and you'll be able to hear as many as 17 different native languages, which include Mapuche, Guaraní and Matacos. Not that you'll be able to recognise any of them, even if you speak Spanish. This means that wherever you go in the city, waiters, tour guides and secret policemen will have a good

excuse for not understanding a word you're saying, and subsequently you can expect your entrée, directions or signed confession to get screwed up.

Eating and Drinking

Buenos Aires boasts some stylish restaurants with waiting staff so arrogant they give the French a run for their money. While Argentinean beef tends to play an important role in the majority of options, non-meat specials are also available, the most popular being a spoonful of over-steamed vegetables on a plate with a cow-sized space left on it.

The uncertain business climate has led to many restaurants being closed down, but new ones are constantly opening in their place. The quality of your meal will tend to be determined by where in the economic cycle your chosen venue is. Expect one of the finest steaks you'll ever eat in a place that's doing OK. Expect a *parrillada* (mixed grill) of stewed intestines and flambéed udder everywhere else.

La Paz

Andean pipe music was discovered here by an elevator designer on annual leave, and is as good a reason for staying away as any.

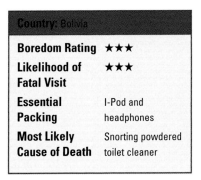

Country: Bolivia

Boredom Rating	★★★
Likelihood of Fatal Visit	★★★
Essential Packing	I-Pod and headphones
Most Likely Cause of Death	Snorting powdered toilet cleaner

History

Despite the presence of some of the friendliest sounding place names in the history of the spoken word, Bolivia's past is a gruesome one. The Incas, famed for lowering the minimum age for human sacrificial victims to, well, zero, were an allegedly ahead-of-their-time but undeniably brutal bunch. They were wiped out by Spanish Conquistadors who were certainly not enlightened and only showed any trace of inventiveness when it came to spending the gold they liberated from the country's many slave-labour-driven mines.

Modern Bolivians have done their best to leave a history of violence behind them by creating a whole new batch of contemporary violence. Military juntas have come and gone like Oprah Winfrey diet regimes, and while the current administration is both democratic and enjoying some kind of popular mandate, the real power lies with those that control the country's illegal coca-plant cultivation – a breed not known for their subtle approach to human relations at the best of times.

Culture

Street life is more important than home life for many La Paz residents, particularly as an unemployment rate as high as the city itself has meant that for a lot more Bolivians the street is now their home. The atmosphere of the city is certainly volatile, and urban unrest is common. This is obviously far from ideal, but it does make a refreshing change from all the rural unrest you'll have encountered getting there in the first place.

Anyone serious about seeing the full breadth of Bolivian culture should consider hiring a guide. Guides can be booked through government-regulated agencies or on the street, but all official guides carry documentation. So, if you become uncertain about your guide, simply ask to see *la autorización*, which guides are instructed to produce on demand. If your guide is unlicensed he will probably produce *una pistola*, and you'll know it's time for you to start saying your *prayeros*.

Attractions

The Witches Market can be found behind the Iglesia de San Francisco and is a good place to pick up traditional confectionery, flick knives and other charms that might offer you an improved chance of surviving your trip.

Charms such as these dried dogs and llamas are said to bring luck to the whole community – except, presumably, the dogs and llamas.

Walking on the Moon

Valle de la Luna is located a short taxi ride from the centre of La Paz, although the bill your driver will present you with would suggest otherwise. This labyrinth of eroded rock formations and not-so-eroded rock formations will, as its name suggests, put you in mind of the light side of the moon, particularly when you add the thin air into the equation. The perfect place to take hyperactive kids you would like to collapse unconscious for a couple of hours.

Llama farmers stage a sit-down protest to demand higher wool prices and the freedom to play pan pipes in European shopping centres.

South of the city, San Vicente is famous for being the place where Butch Cassidy and the Sundance Kid met their maker at the hands of the Bolivian army in 1908. This was the last time the Bolivian authorities were successful in bring any local bandits to justice.

Eating and Drinking

Head into the area between Calle Manco Capac and the Prado for food and your appetite will disappear in no time. Of particular note are the *llajhua*, a spicy sauce that is an excellent treatment for anyone with sinus trouble, and *chichi*, a maize-based liquor that is unique for a drink in that it must be consumed with a knife and fork.

In spring, despite all their best efforts, the local population can do nothing to stop their buses from migrating to the sea.

Mexico City

There's one simple rule to follow if you want to avoid being kidnapped in Mexico City: don't go to Mexico City.

Country:	Mexico
Boredom Rating	★★
Likelihood of Fatal Visit	★★★
Essential Packing	Suitcase full of cash in small, non-sequential bills
Most Likely Cause of Death	Botched exchange

History

As a nightmare of urban sprawl, Mexico City is topped only by Tokyo and New York, and it has had a bloody history even by South American standards. Volcanoes, earthquakes and Aztec initiation ceremonies all played their part in keeping population figures down, and the valley's sole source of water, the Lago de Texcoco, had been shrinking for two millennia by the time an argument over whose turn it was in the bath boiled over into full-on tribal war in the 13th century.

Mexico City started its transformation into the pollution capital of the planet at the turn of the 20th century, when the city's ruling powers embarked on a series of ambitious housing projects in order to accommodate the booming population. Skyscrapers began to appear on the skyline in the 1940s, and while these buildings were seen as highly prestigious addresses for Mexico City residents, the absence of any stairs or elevators made living in them immensely impractical, if not downright hazardous, for everyone except ground-floor residents.

Mexican musicians are notoriously bad at ordering the right size of guitar.

These enraged green VW taxis have spotted a larger VW minibus and moved in for the kill.

Culture

Mexico's culture is what you might expect of a city where even the richest of citizens is never more than a tear-gas-canister's throw from a squalid beggar. Vast differences between rich and poor in the city meant that the crime rate soared during the 1990s, though an allegedly corruption-free administration now claims that it has levelled off in the last two years. So, going to Mexico City is now no more dangerous than participating in a weekend sport such as base jumping, deep-sea freediving or steroid-enhanced bull rodeo.

Attractions

The extent of most people's ambition in Mexico City – other than making it to nightfall with all their fingers – is to win the Lotería Nacional. It is therefore no surprise to find that its Art Deco-styled headquarters are in far better shape than most of the museums, galleries, government buildings and just about everything else that's miraculously still standing in the city.

Eating and Drinking

Mexico City may not have the best restaurants in South America, but it's a great place to go out for dinner with someone whose company you'd prefer to be without. Make sure you're looking your best and

hail one of the distinctive green Volkswagen Beetle taxis on the street. Give your driver the name of an upmarket joint – of which there are about three in Mexico City, the Hilton being the best known – and then let your business competitor/unbearable sibling/adulterous partner get in first before explaining you've forgotten to do something urgent and shutting the door promptly behind them. Head back into your hotel, order a bottle of tequila from room service and wait for the inevitable phone call accompanied by background wailing.

Art of the City

A place the size of Make-Sicko City is bound to produce at least one artist of note, and the suburb of San Angel is where you'll find the Diego Rivera & Frida Kahlo Studio Museum, the Bohemian digs of the famously monobrowed artistic couple. Unfortunately, the gallery's budget has never stretched far enough to allow them to purchase any work by the couple, but at least there's less chance of you getting kidnapped in a crappy gallery than on the space outside where the pavement should be.

Port Stanley

Squaddies, warm beer and a culture based on typical British reserve make this cluster of large rocks in a hostile patch of water one of the most uninteresting places on the planet.

Country: Falkland Islands	
Boredom Rating	★★★★★
Likelihood of Fatal Visit	★★
Essential Packing	Thermal underwear
Most Likely Cause of Death	Unexploded shell, if you're lucky

The splendour and majesty of Her Majesty's Governor's Official (bungalow) Residence.

History

Discovered by Patagonian scouts in rudimentary canoes, the Falkland Islands were declared *visspascuez* (not very nice) by the intrepid seamen, who vowed never to return. As a result, the islands were sensibly uninhabited when Europeans began to frequent the South Atlantic in the 17th century. A British expedition made the first documented landing in 1690 and stayed long enough to plant a flag, name the islands after an underachieving Viscount and notice the large number of penguins before eagerly returning to their boats. The epic discovery was noted in the captain's log between a tirade against the cold weather and an enthusiastic review of the penguin stew the crew had dined on that night.

The high point in the islands' history came in 1774 when the British left and the Spanish moved in and established a penal colony at Port Louis. This remained in operation until the Spanish quit, their last act being to hand a Get Out of Penal Colony Free card to each convict. As a result, the town threatened for the first time to be more heavily populated by humans than penguins as its ranks swelled with whalers, freelance sealers and pirates who'd skipped Introduction to Navigation at Buccaneer college. These violent drunks with dodgy histories welcomed the newly released transportees as kindred spirits.

Culture

The island may well be rich in culture but until we've learnt to communicate with animals we can only speculate as to what it is the penguins like about the place. They would probably tell us that standing on the desolate coast of this windswept and depressing island beats floating in the icy waters of the South Atlantic. And most of the time it probably does. Just.

Attractions

The Falkland Islands are a haven for rare and protected bird life. Unfortunately, this also makes them a priority destination for that most troublesome of breeds, the birdwatcher. The size of the islands will make them difficult to avoid, but look for the tell-tale signs – food stains on clothing, beards (or light moustaches for women) and a penchant for real ale served in a jug – and you can do your best to avoid contact with these social misfits. On a more positive note, the island's 690,000 sheep outnumber the human residents by more than 200 to 1, so you have no excuse for not getting a date on Saturday night.

Eating and Drinking

Port Stanley has the kind of cuisine you'd find in any small British village – none at all. Crisps are sold behind the bar of the islands' pubs, but you are advised to check the sell-by date.

Port-au-Prince

Haiti's golden, sandy beaches, stunning scenery and political volatility have made it the number-one Caribbean destination for members of the United Nations stabilisation force.

Country: Haiti	
Boredom Rating	★
Likelihood of Fatal Visit	★★★★
Essential Packing	Good gris-gris
Most Likely Cause of Death	Voodoo sacrifice to the god of hurricanes

History

Haiti first became populated nearly 5,000 years ago when a drunken bet between two South American tribes on a fishing trip went a little too far. Carried by warm currents into the Caribbean, the hung-over anglers – who presumably had a few women in their party – chose to settle throughout the many islands and gave themselves the name *Taino*, or friendly people. They were certainly friendly to Christopher Columbus on his arrival, sharing with him and the rest of Europe the delights of the hammock, the barbecue and tobacco – three things that have become staples of Western luxury. In the best traditions of European colonisation, the Italian explorer returned the favour by enslaving the native peoples and dragging them off to dig for gold in the hills.

A combination of heavy-handedness with the whip and latent diseases carried by the Spanish slave drivers meant that the majority of the native population was dead within 30 years of Columbus' arrival, at which point the French thought it might be a good idea to get involved. Sick of European interference, Haiti sought independence and became the world's first black republic on January 1st, 1804. The European powers marked Haiti's emergence onto the world stage by doing everything it could to isolate it economically, the effects of which are to be seen on every street of the capital city to this day.

Culture

Haiti has a rich religious heritage, which is evident throughout the city. Unfortunately, there seems to be some disagreement as to which religion it is that is being promoted as the norm. A recent survey found Haiti to be predominantly Catholic, with 80 percent of the population declaring themselves servants of Rome, despite the historical baggage. However, 50 percent of the population also admitted to practising Voodoo, suggesting that either the devotion of the population or the statistical skills of the census takers are questionable at best. This dualism is to be seen in the church architecture, most notably in the Cathedrale de Port-au-Prince where both interior and exterior owe as much to Africa as to Rome, though the resident Bishop draws the line at the positioning of the central crucifix, which he takes personal responsibility for removing the nails from and turning back the right way up after the chapel has been hired out for private ceremonies. Meanwhile, a team of dedicated choirboys is always on hand to mop up any chicken blood that's spurted out as far as the nave.

Attractions

Not surprisingly, given the city's violent past, turbulent present and doubtful future, death looms large in the psyche of the inexplicably cheerful citizens of this squalid city. *Gede* is the biggest festival devoted to it and, although Port-au-Prince is a dangerous town for visitors, it demands to be experienced at street level. Take a wander through the city, look out for black-and-purple-clad devotees of Baron Samedi running up and down the streets excitedly and partying in the city's impressive selection of cemeteries. While this might all sound a little bit intimidating, bear in mind that if you walk onto a street where all the blood-soaked scary people are running around crazily you're probably safe. If they're lying around groaning, you're most likely witnessing community policing at its most hands-on and should get the hell out of there.

You'll probably feel like getting out of the city after a couple of days anyway and Parc Nacional la Visite lies a few miles to the south. The fortress of Sans Souci is an impressive sight. Said to be "impenetrable by man or beast" it proved to be exactly that for its not-so-many years of service before an earthquake wiped it out in 1842. A five-hour hike through some stunning landscape will take you to a rock formation the locals call *Krase Dan*, or broken teeth. Which is precisely what you're likely to be heading home with if you don't take an armed escort with you.

Eating and Drinking

Whatever else you might say about Haiti, it tops the Western Hemispere's charts in two categories – population density and Gross Domestic Product per head (lowest). Still, the restaurants are cheap and cheerful, though the likelihood of a 12-hour blackout could make it worthwhile you ordering dinner 24 hours in advance. Park anywhere in the street and accept the first offer you get to have your car watched. Make sure you're clear about who you've picked for this task by asking their name and pay them five gourds. This will guarantee you get a full description of whoever steals your car, and for an extra five gourds your watcher will usually be happy to tell you which direction the thief drove it off in.

Evil Stepmother Nature

To characterise Haiti as a place beset by purely manmade misery would be totally unrepresentative. For Mother Nature has her part to play in keeping the islanders on their toes too, and the city endures tornadoes and earthquakes like other places suffer from rain showers and traffic jams. In a good year, the Haitian climate might have a shorter than average Hurricane season nestled between two longer than average rainy seasons.

Take your mind off your troubles with Haiti's homely cuisine. *Riz et pois* (rice and peas) has become the national dish and is frequently served alongside pressed plantain, Haiti's own take on the Caribbean staple. What these may lack in interest value they more than make up for in safety-of-stomach value. Meat and fish can be harder to come by, with the exception of chicken claws, which are prevalent on menus. However since Haitian chicken claws tend to enjoy a good ten years of employment between leaving the chicken's leg and making it to your plate, they should be avoided as a rule.

Thankfully for its residents, the city has no need for a visit from TV's Ground Force team, as gardens have been illegal since 1952.

Rio de Janeiro

Tall and tanned and young and lovely she may have been – but if the rest of Rio is anything to go by, the Girl from Ipanema was probably also malnourished, surgically enhanced, living in a one-room shack with her mum and 19 siblings and available by the hour.

Country: Brazil

Boredom Rating	★
Likelihood of Fatal Visit	★★★
Essential Packing	Dental floss/thong
Most Likely Cause of Death	Sloppy anaesthetist

History

Mistakenly labelled a river upon its discovery by a Portuguese explorer who'd had one too many sangrias, Rio de Janeiro was the cause of fierce fighting between the French and Portuguese who both wished to lay claim to its abundance of natural resources – Brazil wood, footballing prowess and crazy Latin rhythms. Despite the fact that the fearsome Tamoio tribes, for reasons best known to them, sided with the French, it was the Portuguese who were victorious, and it was to them that the

Plastic Fantastic

Fortunately, one industry is on the up in Rio. Standards of cosmetic surgery are varied, so it's probably worth taking a few minutes to choose your street-side surgeon before embarking on any procedures, but wherever you go the rates are cheap and the results never less than dramatic. Whether that's a good thing or not will depend on whether you see Alicia Douvall as one of the most beautiful women on the planet or merely an intriguing visitor who seems to have misplaced her ray gun and mother ship.

responsibility fell for ruining another tropical paradise until then untainted by European influences.

One gold rush, a coffee boom and a couple of corny songs later, Rio had become a romantic destination for the in-crowd of the roaring 1920s. Largely unaffected by war, untouched by Prohibition and a no-go area for gossip columnists, it developed a reputation as a town where the rich and ugly or famous but broke could safely exorcise the demons of their hidden lives at knockdown prices, drawing its workforce from the desperate inhabitants of shantytowns so run down that even the rats had dreams of moving out.

The arrival of delegates for the "Eco '92" UN Environmental Conference brought a fresh injection of federal cash, which was spent on road resurfacing for designated routes, floral bouquets for hotel rooms and two-week vacations for the *favelas* muggers, conmen and any prostitutes not in possession of VIP-approval passes. Needless to say, these all had a profound effect on improving the city's environment for the fortnight of the conference, allowing delegates from all over the world to reach several historic agreements about how important it was to try and do something about the state of the ecology at some point in the future before returning to their home states and allowing Rio return to its natural state, that of poverty-stricken *barrio*.

Culture

Malthusian predictions that a geometric population growth would eventually outstrip arithmetic food production have thankfully been proved wrong – largely due to fad diets and the ingenuity of multinationals in producing foods without meat, plant, grain, mineral or any other recognisably nutritious ingredients. But look around the shanties of Rio and you'd think he got it right. There are too many people, yet as individuals there's not enough of them. The only place you're likely to see saggy flesh in Rio is on other tourists or in the mirror in your hotel room, assuming you're lucky enough to be staying in a more upmarket establishment.

Sadly, by-laws concerning thong wear by out-of-towners are rarely enforced by the otherwise heavy-handed Brazilian police. So you can expect your ogling trip to the hugely unfashionable Copacabana beach to be ruined by a combination of self-hatred in contemplation of the figure you must cut among all the skinny locals and utter nausea at the sight of your pasty compatriots wearing swimsuits that look as though they've missed their calling slicing cheese in a delicatessen.

Attractions

A cable car is your best bet for getting to the top of Mount Corcovado to see the statue of *Cristo Redentor* (Christ the Redeemer). Arms held aloft, he begs those in the city below to please try and keep the noise down.

His protestations have no apparent effect, particularly during the five days of carnival every spring where the people of Rio really let their hair down and infectious Latin beats set silicone-enhanced boobs jiggling and well-packed lunchboxes bumping and grinding – frequently on the

same body. Unless you see this as getting the best of both worlds, be very careful who you conga with.

Eating and Drinking

Caipiranhas are sugar rich and sickly enough to put you off the idea of eating altogether, which is just as well considering what else is on offer in Rio.

In the fierce tropical climate many new plants have evolved. This carnivorous *Telephonus gigantica* has lured a tourist into its clutches.

Beaches in Brazil are exclusively reserved for people under 25. Body hair is not allowed, hence the national obsession with "The Brazilian".

San Salvador

El Salvador is a popular global meeting-spot for anyone unafraid of roughing it and working hard to help the country get back on its feet. As a result, it is a highly unsuitable destination for anyone reading this book.

Country: El Salvador	
Boredom Rating	★★★
Likelihood of Fatal Visit	★★
Essential Packing	Rosary beads
Most Likely Cause of Death	Bad mushroom

History

When the Spanish arrived in the region sometime in the 16th century, El Salvador was dominated by the Pipil, a tribe descended from the Aztecs with similar rituals but with less of an emphasis on tequila and human sacrifice and more on herbal tea and group hugs. Mayan influences gave the Pipil a thorough grasp of agriculture, astronomy and mathematics and the Spanish broadened their education with the introduction of slavery and cotton plantations. By the end of the 18th century, the entire country was effectively controlled by a group of 14 European families, who spent most of their time complaining about the insects, the humidity and how difficult it was to find a good wig dresser among the ranks of the indigenous population. Revolution came in 1811, only to think better of the decision and sod off again until the country finally gained independence in 1821. However, Salvadorans were miffed to discover that independence only gave them the right to continue working on the same plantations for the same money (none), and unsuccessful rebellion was followed by disastrous uprising and poorly planned civil disobedience until in 1842 El Salvador finally became an independent sovereign nation and earned itself the right to mess things up on its own. Which it duly did, allowing coffee plantations to remain in the control of an elite minority backed up by a repressive military that lived for the chance to bash heads in. This reached a whole new level in the 1970s and '80s as Death Squads that could teach the CIA a thing or two became the chief tool in community policing and Ronald Reagan helped prop up whichever politicians proved themselves the most right wing.

Culture

While bullets may have ceased flying, Salvadorans remain a jumpy bunch, thanks to a preponderance of backfiring cars, soaring levels of unemployment, mudslides and the sneaking suspicion that, given the country's luck, the many volcanoes that pepper the country's lush landscape are not dormant at all. Not surprisingly, the Catholic Church does brisk business.

Attractions

San Salvador is a bustling market town that is remarkable for the range of items available, particularly as very few people are lucky enough to own anything of any value whatsoever. Still, if you're in the market for textiles woven from donkey hair or crude soft porn painted on the inside of egg shells, head for the Mercado Ex-Cuartel with only as much money as you can afford to lose.

Eating and Drinking

Anyone with an allergy to or dislike for rice and beans may want to think about seeing what the limit is for getting Pot Noodles through customs.

There are many personal shoppers willing to save you the trouble of spending all that cash yourself.

Santo Domingo

A package-deal paradise with a hurricane season timed to coincide with the holiday season. So that's why the travel agent had a guilty look in her eye.

Country: Dominican Republic	
Boredom Rating	★★★
Likelihood of Fatal Visit	★★
Essential Packing	Storm proof clothing
Most Likely Cause of Death	Hurricane whoever

History

With neighbour Haiti a few mere corpse-strewn miles to the west, the Dominican Republic can lay claim to being the least war-ravaged half of the land mass occupied by the two states. Colonised by Spain after Columbus got lucky with his directions in the 16th century, the country's history is the usual jolly Caribbean tale of exploitation of the native inhabitants and oppression and brutality under the hands of European colonial masters until the Europeans got out and allowed the Americans a turn. In 1924, the American Forces finally admitted they had invaded only "because they could" and went home, allowing Horacio Vásquez to become the country's president. The exploitation and oppression of Dominicans has remained a purely domestic affair ever since.

Culture

Santo Domingo has a cultural life that's far healthier than the actual life of anyone who lives there. In addition to some beautifully sound-proofed prison wings, President Rafael Trujillo's great legacy to the city he ruled like a personal fiefdom was without doubt the National School of Fine Arts in the heart of the city. The works within tell the story of Santo Domingo's journey from primitive jungle island to primitive jungle island with a few gale-ravaged hotels on the coast. Due to the somewhat violent history of the country this attraction is not suitable for children.

Attractions

The very best of the city's attractions are to be found on the streets, particularly on Avenida Duarte, Santo Domingo's answer to Times Square, minus any working neon lights. Here you can enjoy the bands on every corner arguing about whether it's a Salsa day or a Merengue day, make a donation to the imaginatively malformed beggars or get a private performance from one of the many street magicians, whose speciality tends to be making your watch and wallet disappear before disappearing themselves. If museums are your thing then the Museo de las Casas Reales (Museum of Broken Dreams) has some of the most filth-encrusted exhibits ever put on display.

Eating and Drinking

If you're staying in Santo Domingo on a package deal, most tour operators will throw full board in with your accommodation. However, if you find the hotel buffet a little bland, be sure to head into one of the many restaurants that dot the city, particularly off the Avenida Duarte. None of them are any good, but this will make you appreciate the hotel's admittedly tasteless fare, and the stomach trouble you're assured to come down with will give you something to focus on next time a member of your party makes the stupid suggestion of leaving the complex.

Some tourists caught out by a light shower.

Picture Acknowledgements

T= Top B= Bottom C=Center R= Right L=Left

©**Chrysalis Image Library:** 63, 68, 69, 97, 122, 123, 158, 164, 165T, 165B.

©**CORBIS:** © Indian Coast Guard/ Handout/ Reuters/ CORBIS 41. / ©Wolfgang Kaehler/ CORBIS 47, 48. / ©Ecole Du Reel /CORBIS SYGMA 57. / ©Tony Arruza/ CORBIS 77. / ©Catherine Karnow/ CORBIS 105. / ©Dean Conger/ CORBIS 110. / ©Mike Blacke/ Reuters/ CORBIS 163. ©Royalty Free / Corbis 176, 177.

©**Digital Vision:** 116.

©**Impact Photos:** 92. / ©Alain Evrard/ Impact Photos 11. / ©Jorn Stjemeklar/ Impact Photos 14. / ©Yann Arthus-Bertrand/ Impact Photos 21, 23. / ©Rupert Conant/ Impact Photos 27, 171. / ©Mike McQueen/ Impact Photos 33. / ©Mark Henley/ Impact Photos 28, 32, 34, 37, 42, 44, 45T, 45B, 70, 99, 102, 111, 184. / ©Ben Edwards/ Impact Photos 36, 149. / ©Piers Cavendish/ Impact Photos 39, 72B, 119, 133, 190. / ©Nigel Amies/ Impact Photos 43. / ©Andy Johnstone/ Impact Photos 62B. / ©Jon Lister/ Impact Photos 62T. / ©John Arthur/ Impact Photos 67. / ©Geraint Lewis/ Impact Photos 71. / ©Jed Leicester/ Impact Photos 75. / ©Jeremy Hunter/ Impact Photos 78. / ©Zute Lightfoot/ Impact Photos 82. / ©Homer Sykes/ Impact Photos 83. / ©Ingolf Pompe/ Impact Photos 87, 91B, 96, 189B. / ©Emile D'Edesse/ Impact Photos 65, 93, 160. / ©Tony Page/ Impact Photos 100. / ©Philip Gordon/ Impact Photos 107T. / ©J Sordet/Ana/ Impact Photos 107B. / ©Toby Key/ Impact Photos 113B. / ©Peter Sofroniou/ Impact Photos 115. / ©Ray Roberts/ Impact Photos 117. / ©Mitch de Faria/ Impact Photos 121. / ©Howard Sayer/ Impact Photos 127. / ©Erol Houssein/ Impact Photos 134, 135. / ©Alan Gignoux/ Impact Photos 137, 151. / ©Robin Laurance/ Impact Photos 138. / ©Caroline Penn/ Impact Photos 142. / ©Alex Macnaughton/ Impact Photos 146. / ©Mohammad Reza Moradabadi/ Impact Photos 150. / ©Ken Graham/ Impact Photos 153. / ©Paul Forster/ Impact Photos 162. / ©Peter Menzel/ Impact Photos 166. / ©Christophe Bluntzer/ Impact Photos 179. / ©Colin Jones / Impact Photos 181. / ©Rhonda Kievansky / Impact Photos 182B. / ©Sergio Dorantes/ Impact Photos 183. / ©David Reed/ Impact Photos 185.

©**Photolibrary.com:** ©Chad Ehlers/ Photolibrary.com 74.

©**Reuters:** ©REUTERS/ Antony Njuguna 10. / ©REUTERS/ Shamil Zhumatoz 26.

©**Rex Features:** ©Jon Santa Cruz/ Rex Features 12. / ©Karl Schoendorfer/ Rex Features 31. / ©Jerry Bergman/ Rex Features 72T. / ©Francis Dean/ Rex Features 73. / ©Armando Dadi/ Rex Features 79. / ©Dimitri Beliakov/ Rex Features 85. / ©Sipa Press/ Rex Features 89T, 147, 175. / ©Graham Trott/ Rex Features 89B. / ©Martin McCullough/ Rex Features 95. / ©Isopress Senepart/ Rex Features 101. / ©Guzelian Photos/ Rex Features 103. / ©The Travel Library/ Rex Features 125. / ©David Hartley/ Rex Features 129. / ©Haitham Moussawi/ Rex Features 143. / ©MAI/ Rex Features 145. / ©Heather Coulson/ Rex Features 148. / ©Images/ Rex Features 155. / ©Rex USA Ltd / Rex Features 174. / ©Dan Callister/ Rex Features 191.

©**Still Pictures:** 15. / ©Ludger Schadomsky/ Still Pictures 17. / ©Julio Etchart / Still Pictures 19, 189T. / ©Jean-Leo Dugast/ Still Pictures 29, 30. / ©Jorgen Schytte/ Still Pictures 38. / ©Nigel Dickinson/ Still Pictures 49. / ©Carolyn Johns / Still Pictures 51, 52. / ©Friedrich Stark / Still Pictures 55. / ©Martin Wyness/ Still Pictures 59. / ©Pierre Gleizes/ Still Pictures 81. / ©Paco Feria/ Still Pictures 91T. / ©Sebastian Bolesch/ Still Pictures 94. / ©A. Riedmiller/ Still Pictures 90, 108, 109. / ©Jochen Tack/ Still Pictures 113T. / ©Ron Giling/ Still Pictures 131, 180. / ©Donald Bostrom/ Still Pictures 140. / ©Johann Scheibner/ Still Pictures 141. / ©Jeff Greenberg/ Still Pictures 157. / ©Mark Edwards/ Still Pictures 167. / ©Peter Frischmuth/ Still Pictures 53, 169, 173. / ©Charlotte Thege/ Still Pictures 182T. / ©Pascale Simard/ Still Pictures 187.

Main front cover image: © Steve Austin Papilio/CORBIS / TL: © Ashley Cooper/CORBIS / TC: © Peter Turnley/CORBIS / TR: © Paul A. Souders/CORBIS / BR: © Baci/CORBIS / Main back cover image: © Stockbyte